Kivy Blueprints

Build your very own app-store-ready, multi-touch games and applications with Kivy!

Mark Vasilkov

open source*
community experience distilled

BIRMINGHAM - MUMBAI

Kivy Blueprints

First published: January 2015

Production reference: 1230115

Published by Packt Publishing Ltd.
Livery Place
35 Livery Street
Birmingham B3 2PB, UK.

ISBN 978-1-78398-784-9

www.packtpub.com

Credits

Author
Mark Vasilkov

Reviewers
Takumi Adachi
Joe Dorocak
Raphael Pierzina
Edward C. Delaporte V

Commissioning Editor
Usha Iyer

Acquisition Editor
Vinay Argekar

Content Development Editor
Kirti Patil

Technical Editors
Arwa Manasawala
Rahul Shah

Copy Editors
Roshni Banerjee
Gladson Monteiro
Karuna Narayanan

Project Coordinator
Nidhi Joshi

Proofreaders
Martin Diver
Maria Gould
Paul Hindle
Joanna McMahon

Indexers
Hemangini Bari
Rekha Nair
Priya Subramani

Graphics
Sheetal Aute

Production Coordinator
Nilesh R. Mohite

Cover Work
Nilesh R. Mohite

About the Author

Mark Vasilkov is a software craftsman—or engineer—whichever you prefer. He specializes in Python and JavaScript development, mostly related to web and mobile applications, and has 10 years of experience in hacking stuff together so that it mostly works.

For what it's worth, Mark is a Russian Israeli. This very book was partially written in a bomb shelter due to Hamas shooting long-range rockets (containing warheads with up to 200 kg explosives each) at Tel Aviv. Israel is a beautiful country, inspiring everyone in the region to do something truly remarkable and idiosyncratic.

About the Reviewers

Takumi Adachi is currently working as an Android developer for Applocation based in Victoria, British Columbia, Canada. He enjoys programming, kendo, cycling, and video games. He is a proponent for open source and strictly uses the MIT license for his personal projects and code. He specializes in Java, Python, JavaScript, and web markup languages such as HTML and CSS. He is exposed to a wide range of technologies such as JavaScript, Python, HTML, CSS, SQL, SQLite, Vagrant, AngularJS, PHP, node.js, Git, REST, JSON, Bash, Linux, OS X, Windows, nginx, VirtualBox, Visual Studio 2013, Java, Excel, Android, and so on.

He has helped review the book, *Kivy Blueprints,* and hopes to continue reviewing books for Packt Publishing.

> I would like to thank my cousin, Justin, parents, teachers, and employers for providing me with opportunities to grow and develop, and supporting me in my endeavors.

Joe Dorocak, whose Internet moniker is Joe Codeswell, is a very experienced programmer. He enjoys creating readable code that implements the project requirements efficiently and understandably. He considers writing code akin to writing poetry.

He prides himself on the ability to communicate clearly and professionally. He considers his code to be communication, not only with the machine platforms upon which it will run, but with all those human programmers who will read it in the future.

He has been employed either as a direct employee or as a contractor by IBM, HP, GTE/Sprint, and other top-shelf companies. He is presently concentrating on app and web project consulting, coded primarily, but not exclusively, in Python and JavaScript. For more details, please check Joe's LinkedIn profile at `https://www.linkedin.com/in/joedorocak`.

Raphael Pierzina is currently working as a development lead at Mackevision (`http://mackevision.com/`) in Germany. He is responsible for a Python/PySide-based standalone application for defining and managing complex configuration logic data sets for data-based visualization in terms of code reviews and supervision. He holds a bachelor's degree in virtual design and specializes in computer graphics and interactive applications.

Raphael is passionate about idiomatic Python code and development techniques such as TDD. He enjoys contributing to open source projects such as Cookiecutter (`https://github.com/audreyr/cookiecutter`) and occasionally posts on his personal blog (`http://www.hackebrot.de/`) about various topics, including MaxScript, comic books, and his adventures in the world of Linux.

> I would like to thank my loving family and my close friends for their support over the course of this project. Thank you for your understanding when I had little time to spare. I wish to express my gratitude to the team at Packt Publishing for providing me with the opportunity to be a part of this amazing book.

Edward C. Delaporte V leads a software development group at the University of Illinois and has contributed to the documentation of the Kivy framework. He is thankful to all those whose contributions to the open source community made his career possible, and he hopes this book helps to attract enthusiasts to software development.

www.PacktPub.com

Support files, eBooks, discount offers, and more

For support files and downloads related to your book, please visit www.PacktPub.com.

Did you know that Packt offers eBook versions of every book published, with PDF and ePub files available? You can upgrade to the eBook version at www.PacktPub.com and as a print book customer, you are entitled to a discount on the eBook copy. Get in touch with us at service@packtpub.com for more details.

At www.PacktPub.com, you can also read a collection of free technical articles, sign up for a range of free newsletters, and receive exclusive discounts and offers on Packt books and eBooks.

https://www2.packtpub.com/books/subscription/packtlib

Do you need instant solutions to your IT questions? PacktLib is Packt's online digital book library. Here, you can search, access, and read Packt's entire library of books.

Why subscribe?

- Fully searchable across every book published by Packt
- Copy and paste, print, and bookmark content
- On demand and accessible via a web browser

Free access for Packt account holders

If you have an account with Packt at www.PacktPub.com, you can use this to access PacktLib today and view 9 entirely free books. Simply use your login credentials for immediate access.

To my wife, Natalia

Table of Contents

Preface

Mobile applications ceased to be the "new hotness" a long time ago, and these days users routinely expect that new software—be it a videogame or a social network—has a mobile version. Similar trend affects desktop operating systems; writing cross-platform software, once uncommon, has swiftly become a norm. Even game developers, usually limited to Microsoft operating systems on desktop, can be seen working on Mac and Linux ports for many new titles (for example, Steam, at the time of writing, hosts more than a hundred games that run on Mac and more than 50 that run on Linux).

This is especially valuable for start-ups and indie developers: building truly cross-platform software widens the potential audience, which leads to increased sales and may create good press along the way.

On the downside, writing portable software can be a very resource-hungry process, and this also affects small developers much more than big corporations.

In particular, many platforms have a preferred programming language and **software development kit** (**SDK**): iOS apps are mostly written in Objective-C and Swift, Android suggests the subpar Java programming language, and Microsoft promotes the use of the .NET framework, especially C#, for building Windows software.

Employing these tools allows you to leverage the native user interface and underlying functionality of an OS, but it also automatically prevents code reuse. This means that even if you are equally proficient in all programming languages and interfaces involved, porting the code may still take a non-trivial amount of time and introduce new bugs.

Write once, run anywhere

This whole situation creates a demand for a universal, multi-platform way to program. The problem isn't exactly new: one solution to it, created by Sun in 1995, is the Java programming language. Its marketing promise — *write once, run anywhere* — was never fulfilled and the language itself is unreasonably cumbersome to use. This led to many mocking variations of the slogan, culminating with *write once, run away* that refers to many developers abandoning Java in favor of better programming languages, including Python.

Not coincidentally, Kivy — the main topic of this book — is a graphical user interface library facilitating easy creation of multi-platform Python applications. The main features of Kivy toolkit are as follows:

- **Compatibility**: Kivy-based apps work in Linux, Mac OS X, Windows, Android, and iOS — all from a single codebase.

- **Natural user interface**: Kivy bridges the gap between different input methods, allowing you to handle a multitude of possible user interactions with similar code, mouse events and multitouch gestures alike.

- **Fast hardware-accelerated graphics**: OpenGL rendering makes Kivy suitable for creating graphics-heavy applications such as videogames, and also improves the user experience with smooth transitions.

- **The use of Python**: Kivy apps are written in Python, one of the better general purpose programming languages. In addition to being inherently portable, expressive, and readable, Python features a useful standard library and a rich ecosystem of third-party packages, the **Python Package Index (PyPI)**.

Speaking of third-party packages, Kivy can be seen as a superset of many battle-tested components: a large part of its functionality relies on well-known libraries such as Pygame, SDL, and GStreamer. The API that Kivy exposes, however, is very high-level and unified.

It's worth mentioning that Kivy is free and open source MIT licensed software. In practice, this means that you can use it commercially without paying licensing fees. Its full source code is hosted on GitHub, so you can also patch bugs or add new features to it.

What this book covers

Chapter 1, Building a Clock App provides a gentle introduction to writing applications with Kivy. It covers the Kivy language, layouts, widgets and timers. By the end of the chapter we build a simple Clock app, similar to the one found in your cellphone.

Chapter 2, *Building a Paint App* is a further exploration of the Kivy framework's components and functionality. The resulting Paint app showcases the customization of built-in widgets, drawing arbitrary shapes on canvas and handling multi-touch events.

Chapter 3, *Sound Recorder for Android* serves as an example of writing a Kivy-based Android app. It shows how to use the Pyjnius interoperability layer to load Java classes into Python, which enables us to mix Android API calls with a Kivy-based user interface.

Chapter 4, *Kivy Networking* is a hands-on guide to building a network application from the ground up. In covers a number of topics, from creating a simple protocol to writing server and client software in Python, and culminates with the Kivy Chat application.

Chapter 5, *Making a Remote Desktop App* exemplifies another way of writing client-server apps. This chapter's program is based on the HTTP protocol—the one that powers the Internet. We develop a command-line HTTP server first, and then build the Remote Desktop client app with Kivy.

Chapter 6, *Making the 2048 Game* walks you through building a playable replica of the 2048 game. We demonstrate more complex Kivy functionality, such as creating custom widgets, using Kivy properties for data binding, and processing touch screen gestures.

Chapter 7, *Writing a Flappy Bird Clone* introduces another Kivy-based game, this time it's an arcade game similar to the well-known Flappy Bird title. Over the course of this chapter we discuss the use of texture coordinates and sounds effects, implement arcade physics and collision detection.

Chapter 8, *Introducing Shaders* demonstrates the use of GLSL shaders in the context of a Kivy application. In this tutorial you will learn about OpenGL primitives such as indices and vertices, and then write incredibly fast low-level code that runs directly on the GPU.

Chapter 9, *Making a Shoot-Em-Up Game* continues where the previous chapter left off: we use the knowledge of GLSL in order to build a side-scrolling shooter. A reusable particle system class is developed along the way. This project concludes the series and capitalizes on many techniques that were explained throughout the book, such as collision detection, touch screen controls, sound effects and so on.

Appendix, *The Python Ecosystem*, gives you more on Python libraries and tools.

Setting up the working environment

This section briefly discusses the requirements needed to effectively follow the narrative, implement, and run Kivy applications. Personal computer running a modern operating system—a Mac, Linux, or Windows box—is implied.

A note on Python

Python is the primary programming language used in the book; good knowledge of it, while not strictly necessary, may help.

At the time of writing, there are two incompatible versions of Python in wide use. Python 2.7 is monumentally stable but no longer actively developed, and Python 3 is a newer and slightly more controversial version bringing many improvements to the language, but occasionally breaking compatibility along the way.

The code in this book should largely work in both Python versions, but it may need minor adjustments to be fully compatible with Python 3; for best results, it's recommended that you use Python 2.7, or the latest Python 2 version available for your system.

> Installing Python separately for Kivy development is not necessary on most platforms: it either comes preinstalled (Mac OS X), bundled with Kivy (MS Windows), or included as a dependency (Linux, Ubuntu in particular).

Installing and running Kivy

Kivy can be downloaded from the official site (`http://kivy.org/`); just choose an appropriate version and follow the instructions. This whole procedure should be pretty straightforward and simple.

Operating System	File	Instructions	Size
Windows 7, 8 (32/64 bit)	Kivy-1.8.0-py2.7-win32.zip (Mirror) Kivy-1.8.0-py3.3-win32.zip (Mirror)	Installation for Windows	126MB 129MB
Mac OS X 10.7, 10.8, 10.9 (requires Python 2.7)	Kivy-1.8.0-osx.dmg (Mirror)	Installation for MacOSX	34 Mb
Linux (tested Ubuntu > 13.04, 32/64 bit, Maegia, Arch)	Kivy-1.8.0.tar.gz	Installation for Ubuntu	13 Mb

Kivy downloads

To check whether the installation is working, follow these instructions:

- On a Mac:

    1. Open **Terminal.app**.

    2. Run `kivy`.

    3. The Python prompt, `>>>`, should appear. Type `import kivy`.

    4. The command should complete with no errors, printing a message along the lines of `[INFO] Kivy v1.8.0`.

- On a Linux machine:

    1. Open a terminal.

    2. Run `python`.

    3. The Python prompt, `>>>`, should appear. Type `import kivy`.

    4. The command should print a message similar to `[INFO] Kivy v1.8.0`.

- On a Windows box:

    1. Double-click **kivy.bat** inside the Kivy package directory.

    2. Type `python` at the command prompt.

    3. Type `import kivy`.

    4. The command should print a message similar to `[INFO] Kivy v1.8.0`.

```
(~) kivy
Python 2.7.5 (default, Mar  9 2014, 22:15:05)
[GCC 4.2.1 Compatible Apple LLVM 5.0 (clang-500.0.68)] on darwin
Type "help", "copyright", "credits" or "license" for more information.
>>> import kivy
[INFO              ] Kivy v1.8.0
>>>
```

A terminal session

Running a Kivy application (basically, a Python program) is achieved similarly:

- On a Mac, use `kivy main.py`
- On Linux, use `python main.py`
- On Windows, use `kivy.bat main.py` (or drag-and-drop the **main.py** file on top of **kivy.bat**).

Note on coding

Programming typically amounts to working with text a lot; hence, it's important to choose a good text editor. This is why I profoundly recommend trying Vim before you consider other options.

Vim is one of the better text editors largely available; it's highly configurable and built specifically for effective text editing (way more so than a typical alternative). Vim has a vibrant community, is actively maintained, and comes preinstalled with many Unix-like operating systems—including Mac OS X and Linux. It is known that (at least some) developers of the Kivy framework also prefer Vim.

Here are some quick Kivy-related tips for Vim users out there:

- **Python-mode** (`https://github.com/klen/python-mode`) is great for writing Python code. It throws in a lot of extra functionality, such as stylistic and static checker, smart completion, and support for refactoring.

- Source code of GLSL shaders can be properly highlighted using the `vim-glsl` syntax (`https://github.com/tikhomirov/vim-glsl`).

- Kivy texture maps (the `.atlas` files, covered in *Chapter 8, Introducing Shaders*) are basically JSON, so you can use, for example, **vim-json** (`https://github.com/elzr/vim-json`), and add a file association to your `.vimrc` file like this:

  ```
  au BufNewFile,BufRead *.atlas set filetype=json
  ```

- Kivy layout files, `.kv`, are slightly more complicated to handle as they're similar to Python, but don't really parse as Python. There is an incomplete Vim plugin in the Kivy repository, but at the time of writing, Vim's built-in **YAML** support highlights these files better (this obviously might change in future). To load `.kv` files as YAML, add the following line to your `.vimrc` file:

  ```
  au BufNewFile,BufRead *.kv set filetype=yaml
  ```

Clearly, you are not *obliged* to use Vim to follow examples of this book—this is but a mere suggestion. Now let's write a bit of code, shall we?

Hello, Kivy

When learning a new programming language or technology, the first thing demonstrated to students is traditionally a "hello, world" program. This is how it looks in Python:

```
print('hello, world')
```

The Kivy version of a "hello, world" is a little lengthier and consists of two files, namely, a Python module and a .kv layout definition.

Code

A Kivy application's entry point is customarily called main.py, and its contents are as follows:

```
from kivy.app import App

class HelloApp(App):
    pass

if __name__ == '__main__':
    HelloApp().run()
```

As you can see, this takes Kivy's App class, adds absolutely nothing to it, and calls run().

Layout

A layout file is typically named after the application class, in this case HelloApp, sans the App suffix and in lowercase: hello.kv. It contains the following lines:

```
Label:
    text: 'Hello, Kivy'
```

This is a very simple Kivy layout definition consisting of a single widget, Label, with the desired text inside. Layout files allow building complex widget hierarchies in a concise, declarative fashion, which is clearly not displayed here, but will be heavily used over the course of this book.

If we run the program now (refer to the *Installing and running Kivy* section for details), this is what we'll get:

Our first application powered by Kivy

Now you're ready to move on to the first chapter and start writing real programs.

Who this book is for

This book is intended for programmers who are comfortable with the Python language and who want to build desktop and mobile applications with a rich graphical user interface in Python with minimal hassle. Knowledge of Kivy, while certainly won't hurt, is not required—every aspect of the framework is described when it's first used.

At various points in this book, we will make an analogy between Kivy and web development practices. However, an extensive knowledge of the latter also isn't required to follow the narrative.

Conventions

In this book, you will find a number of text styles that distinguish between different kinds of information. Here are some examples of these styles and an explanation of their meaning.

Code words in text, database table names, folder names, filenames, file extensions, pathnames, dummy URLs, user input, and Twitter handles are shown as follows: "Kivy application's entry point is customarily called `main.py`."

A block of code is set as follows:

```
from kivy.app import App

class HelloApp(App):
    pass

if __name__ == '__main__':
    HelloApp().run()
```

When we wish to draw your attention to a particular part of a code block, the relevant lines or items are set in bold:

```
# In Python code
LabelBase.register(name="Roboto",
    fn_regular="Roboto-Regular.ttf",
    fn_bold="Roboto-Bold.ttf",
    fn_italic="Roboto-Italic.ttf",
    fn_bolditalic="Roboto-BoldItalic.ttf")
```

Any command-line input or output is written as follows:

```
pip install -U twisted
```

New terms and **important words** are shown in bold. Words that you see on the screen, for example, in menus or dialog boxes, appear in the text like this: "The first event handler is for the **Start** and **Stop** buttons."

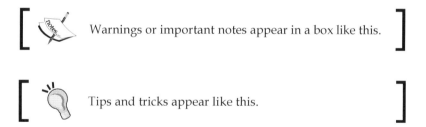

Warnings or important notes appear in a box like this.

Tips and tricks appear like this.

Reader feedback

Feedback from our readers is always welcome. Let us know what you think about this book—what you liked or disliked. Reader feedback is important for us as it helps us develop titles that you will really get the most out of.

To send us general feedback, simply e-mail feedback@packtpub.com, and mention the book's title in the subject of your message.

If there is a topic that you have expertise in and you are interested in either writing or contributing to a book, see our author guide at `www.packtpub.com/authors`.

Customer support

Now that you are the proud owner of a Packt book, we have a number of things to help you to get the most from your purchase.

Downloading the example code

You can download the example code files from your account at `http://www.packtpub.com` for all the Packt Publishing books you have purchased. If you purchased this book elsewhere, you can visit `http://www.packtpub.com/support` and register to have the files e-mailed directly to you. Another option of getting the up-to-date source code is by cloning the GitHub repository, `https://github.com/mvasilkov/kb`.

Downloading the color images of this book

We also provide you with a PDF file that has color images of the screenshots/diagrams used in this book. The color images will help you better understand the changes in the output. You can download this file from: `http://www.packtpub.com/sites/default/files/downloads/7849OS_ColorImages.pdf`.

Errata

Although we have taken every care to ensure the accuracy of our content, mistakes do happen. If you find a mistake in one of our books — maybe a mistake in the text or the code — we would be grateful if you could report this to us. By doing so, you can save other readers from frustration and help us improve subsequent versions of this book. If you find any errata, please report them by visiting `http://www.packtpub.com/submit-errata`, selecting your book, clicking on the **Errata Submission Form** link, and entering the details of your errata. Once your errata are verified, your submission will be accepted and the errata will be uploaded to our website or added to any list of existing errata under the Errata section of that title.

To view the previously submitted errata, go to `https://www.packtpub.com/books/content/support` and enter the name of the book in the search field. The required information will appear under the **Errata** section.

Piracy

Piracy of copyrighted material on the Internet is an ongoing problem across all media. At Packt, we take the protection of our copyright and licenses very seriously. If you come across any illegal copies of our works in any form on the Internet, please provide us with the location address or website name immediately so that we can pursue a remedy.

Please contact us at copyright@packtpub.com with a link to the suspected pirated material.

We appreciate your help in protecting our authors and our ability to bring you valuable content.

Questions

If you have a problem with any aspect of this book, you can contact us at questions@packtpub.com, and we will do our best to address the problem.

1
Building a Clock App

This book will walk you through the creation of nine little Kivy programs, each resembling a real-world use case for the Kivy framework. On many occasions, the framework will be utilized together with other Python modules fitting for the task at hand. We will see that Kivy provides a great deal of flexibility, allowing us to solve vastly different problems in a clean, concise manner.

Let's start small. In this chapter, we will build a simple Clock app, similar in concept to the built-in application found in both iOS and Android. In the first part of the chapter, we will create a non-interactive digital clock display and style it, giving our program an Android-ish flat look. We will also briefly discuss the event-driven program flow and a Kivy main loop, introducing timers used to perform recurring tasks, such as updating the screen every frame.

In the second part of this chapter, we will add a stopwatch display and controls, creating a fluid layout suitable for any screen size and orientation. A stopwatch, naturally, needs user interaction, which we are going to implement last.

The important topics introduced in this chapter are as follows:

- The basics of the Kivy language, a built-in **domain-specific language** (DSL) used to lay out widgets
- Styling (and eventually subclassing) built-in Kivy components
- Loading custom fonts and formatting text
- Scheduling and listening to events

Our finished program, depicted in the following screenshot, will only be about 60 lines long, split equally between a Python source code and a Kivy language (.kv) interface definition file.

The final look of the Clock app we're going to build.

The starting point

Our "Hello, Kivy" example from the preface is a suitable starting point for this app. We just need to add a layout container, BoxLayout, so that we can fit more than one widget on the screen later.

This is the full source code at this point:

```python
# File: main.py
from kivy.app import App

class ClockApp(App):
    pass

if __name__ == '__main__':
    ClockApp().run()

# File: clock.kv
BoxLayout:
    orientation: 'vertical'

    Label:
        text: '00:00:00'
```

Right now, it looks and behaves exactly like the previously seen "Hello, world" app. A `BoxLayout` container allows two or more child widgets to coexist side by side, stacking either vertically or horizontally. Given just one nested widget, as in the preceding code, `BoxLayout` fills up all the available screen space with it and thus becomes practically unnoticeable (it's as if `Label` was a root widget instead, taking over the application window). We will review layouts in more detail later on.

> Note that while we may call the `main.py` file anything we want, the `clock.kv` file is autoloaded by Kivy, and therefore, has to be named after the application class. For example, if our app class is called `FooBarApp`, a corresponding `.kv` file should be named `foobar.kv` (the class name converted to lowercase and without the `-app` suffix). Closely following this naming convention allows us to avoid loading Kivy language files manually, which is unequivocally a good thing—less lines of code leading to the same result.

Modern UI

At the time of writing this, the flat design paradigm is trending in the interface design field, systematically taking over every platform, be it Web, mobile, or desktop. Prominent examples of this paradigm shift in the wild are iOS 7 and later and Windows 8 and later. Internet companies followed suit with the "Material design principles" presented at Google I/O 2014 conference, along with many other HTML5 frameworks, including the well-established ones, for example, Bootstrap.

Conveniently, the flat design emphasizes content over presentation, omitting photo-realistic shadows and detailed textures in favor of plain colors and simple geometry. It is by all means simpler to create programmatically than the "old school" skeuomorphic design that tends to be visually rich and artistic.

> **Skeuomorphism** is a common approach to user interface design. It is characterized by applications visually imitating their real-world counterparts, for example, a Calculator app with the same button layout and look and feel as a cheap physical calculator. This may or may not help user experience (depending on who you ask).

Giving up visual details in favor of a simpler, more streamlined interface seems to be the direction everyone is going in today. On the other hand, it's naturally challenging to build a distinctive, memorable interface just from colored rectangles and such. This is why the flat design is typically synonymous with good typography; depending on the application, text is almost always a significant part of the UI, so we want it to look great.

Design inspiration

Imitation is the sincerest form of flattery, and we will imitate the clock design from Android 4.1 Jelly Bean. The distinctive feature of this design is the font weight contrast. Until it was changed in version 4.4 KitKat, the default clock used to look like this:

Clock in Jelly Bean flavor of Android, as seen on the lock screen.

The font used is Roboto, Google's Android font that superseded the Droid font family in Android 4.0 Ice Cream Sandwich.

Roboto is free for commercial use and available under the permissive Apache License. It can be downloaded from Google Fonts or from the excellent Font Squirrel library at `http://www.fontsquirrel.com/fonts/roboto`.

Loading custom fonts

When it comes to the typography, Kivy defaults to Droid Sans—Google's earlier font. It's easy to replace Droid with a custom font, as Kivy allows us to specify the `font_name` property for textual widgets (in this case, `Label`).

In the simplest case when we have just one font variant, it is possible to assign a `.ttf` filename directly in the definition of a widget:

```
Label:
    font_name: 'Lobster.ttf'
```

For the aforementioned design, however, we want different font weights, so this approach won't cut it. The reason being, every variation of a font (for example, bold or italic) commonly lives in a separate file, and we can only assign one filename to the `font_name` property.

Our use case, involving more than one `.ttf` file, is better covered by a `LabelBase.register` static method. It accepts the following arguments (all optional), exemplified by the Roboto font family:

```
# In Python code
LabelBase.register(name="Roboto",
    fn_regular="Roboto-Regular.ttf",
    fn_bold="Roboto-Bold.ttf",
    fn_italic="Roboto-Italic.ttf",
    fn_bolditalic="Roboto-BoldItalic.ttf")
```

After this invocation, it becomes possible to set the `font_name` property of a widget to the name of the previously registered font family, `Roboto` in this case.

This approach has two limitations to be aware of:

- Kivy only accepts TrueType `.ttf` font files. If the fonts are packaged as OpenType `.otf` or a web font format such as `.woff`, you may need to convert them first. This can be easily done using the FontForge editor, which can be found at `http://fontforge.org/`.

- There is a maximum of four possible styles per font: normal, italic, bold, and bold italic. It's fine for older font families, such as Droid Sans, but many modern fonts include anywhere from 4 to over 20 styles with varying font weight and other features. Roboto, which we're going to use shortly, is available in at least 12 styles.

Roboto Thin	**Roboto Medium**
Roboto Light	**Roboto Bold**
Roboto Normal	**Roboto Ultra-Bold**

The six font weights of Roboto font

The second point forces us to choose which font styles we will use in our application as we can't just throw in all 12, which is a bad idea anyway as it would lead to a hefty increase in file size, up to 1.7 megabytes in the case of Roboto family.

For this particular app, we only need two styles: a lighter one (`Roboto-Thin.ttf`) and a heavier one (`Roboto-Medium.ttf`), which we assign to `fn_regular` and `fn_bold` respectively:

```
from kivy.core.text import LabelBase

LabelBase.register(name='Roboto',
                   fn_regular='Roboto-Thin.ttf',
                   fn_bold='Roboto-Medium.ttf')
```

This code should be placed right after the `__name__ == '__main__'` line in `main.py`, as it needs to run before the interface is created from the Kivy language definition. By the time the app class is instantiated, it might already be too late to perform basic initialization like this. This is why we have to do it in advance.

Now that we have a custom font in place, all that's left is to assign it to our `Label` widget. This can be done with the help of the following code:

```
# In clock.kv
Label:
    text: '00:00:00'
    font_name: 'Roboto'
    font_size: 60
```

Formatting text

The most popular and universally used markup language out there is undoubtedly HTML. Kivy, on the other hand, implements a variant of BBCode, a markup language once used to format posts on many message boards. Visible distinction from HTML is that BBCode uses square brackets as tag delimiters.

The following tags are available in Kivy:

BBCode tag	Effect on text
`[b]...[/b]`	**Bold**
`[i]...[/i]`	*Italic*
`[font=Lobster]...[/font]`	Change font
`[color=#FF0000]...[/color]`	Set color with CSS-like syntax
`[sub]...[/sub]`	Subscript (text below the line)
`[sup]...[/sup]`	Superscript (text above the line)
`[ref=name]...[/ref]`	Clickable zone, `<a href="...">` in HTML
`[anchor=name]`	Named location, `<a name="...">` in HTML

This is by no means an exhaustive reference because Kivy is under active development and has probably undergone a number of releases since this text was written, adding new features and refining the existing functionality. Please refer to the Kivy documentation found on the official website (`http://kivy.org`) for an up-to-date reference manual.

Let's return to our project. To achieve the desired formatting (hours in bold and the rest of the text in fn_regular thin font), we can use the following code:

```
Label:
    text: '[b]00[/b]:00:00'
    markup: True
```

Kivy's BBCode flavor works only if we also set the markup property of a widget to True, as shown in the preceding code. Otherwise, you will literally see the string [b]...[/b] displayed on the screen, and that's clearly not desired.

Note that if we wanted to make the whole text bold, there is no need to enclose everything in [b]...[/b] tags; we could just set the bold property of the widget to True. The same applies to italic, color, font name, and size—pretty much everything can be configured globally to affect the whole widget without touching markup.

Changing the background color

In this section, we will adjust the window background color. Window background (the "clear color" of OpenGL renderer) is a property of a global Window object. In order to change it, we add this code right after the __name__ == '__main__' line in main.py:

```
from kivy.core.window import Window
from kivy.utils import get_color_from_hex

Window.clearcolor = get_color_from_hex('#101216')
```

The get_color_from_hex function is not strictly required, but it's nice as it allows us to use CSS-style (#RRGGBB) colors instead of (R, G, B) tuples throughout our code. And using CSS colors is preferable for at least the following two reasons:

- **Less cognitive overhead when reading**: The #FF0080 value is immediately recognized as a color when you're familiar with this notation, while (255, 0, 128) is just a bunch of numbers that may be used differently depending on the context. The floating-point variant of #FF0080, (1.0, 0.0, 0.50196) is even worse.

- **Simple and unambiguous searching**: A tuple can be arbitrarily formatted, while a CSS-like color notation is uniform, albeit case-insensitive. Performing a case-insensitive search in most text editors is very simple, as opposed to locating all instances of a given tuple inside a lengthy Python listing. The latter task can prove challenging and involve regular expressions, among other things, because the formatting of tuples doesn't have to be consistent.

More information about the #RRGGBB color format can be found on Mozilla Developer Network at `https://developer.mozilla.org/en-US/docs/Web/Guide/CSS/Getting_started/Color`.

We will talk more about design-related features of Kivy later on. Meanwhile, let's make our application actually show the time.

Making the clock tick

UI frameworks are mostly event-driven, and Kivy is no exception. The distinction from the "usual" procedural code is simple—the event-driven code needs to return to the main loop often; otherwise, it will be unable to process events from a user (such as pointer movement, clicks, or window resize), and the interface will "freeze." If you're a longtime Microsoft Windows user, you are probably familiar with programs that are unresponsive and freeze very often. It is crucial to never let this happen in our apps.

Practically, this means that we can't just code an infinite loop like this in our program:

```
# Don't do this
while True:
    update_time()  # some function that displays time
    sleep(1)
```

Technically, it might work, but the application's UI will stay in the "not responding" state until the application gets killed (forcefully stopped) by the user or an operating system. Instead of taking this faulty approach, we need to keep in mind that there is a main loop running inside Kivy, and we need to take advantage of it by utilizing events and timers.

Event-driven architecture also means that in many places, we will listen to events to respond to various conditions, be it user input, network events, or timeouts.

One of the common events that many programs listen to is `App.on_start`. A method with this name, if defined on the application class, will be called as soon as the app is fully initialized. Another good example of an event that we will find in many programs is `on_press`, which fires when the user clicks, taps, or otherwise interacts with a button.

Speaking of time and timers, we can easily schedule our code to run in the future using a built-in `Clock` class. It exposes the following static methods:

- `Clock.schedule_once`: Runs a function once after a timeout
- `Clock.schedule_interval`: Runs a function periodically

 Anyone with a JavaScript background will easily recognize these two functions. They are exactly like `window.setTimeout` and `window.setInterval` in JS. Indeed, the Kivy programming model is very similar to JavaScript even if the API looks completely different.

It's important to understand that all timed events that originate from `Clock` run as a part of Kivy's main event loop. This approach is not synonymous to threading, and scheduling a blocking function like this may prevent other events from being invoked in a timely manner, or at all.

Updating the time on the screen

To access the `Label` widget that holds time, we will give it a unique identifier (`id`). Later, we can easily look up widgets based on their `id` property—again, a concept which is very similar to web development.

Modify `clock.kv` by adding the following:

```
Label:
    id: time
```

That's it! Now we can access this `Label` widget from our code directly using the `root.ids.time` notation (`root` in our case is `BoxLayout`).

Updates to the `ClockApp` class include the addition of a method to display time, `update_time`, which looks like this:

```
def update_time(self, nap):
    self.root.ids.time.text = strftime('[b]%H[/b]:%M:%S')
```

Now let's schedule the update function to run once per second after the program starts:

```
def on_start(self):
    Clock.schedule_interval(self.update_time, 1)
```

If we run the application right now, we'll see that the time displayed is being updated every second. To paraphrase Neil Armstrong, that is one small step for mankind, but a sizable leap for a Kivy beginner.

It's worth noting how the argument to strftime combines Kivy's BBCode-like tags described earlier with the function-specific C-style format directives. For the unfamiliar, here's a quick and incomplete reference on strftime formatting essentials:

Format string (case-sensitive)	Resulting output
%S	Second as two digits, typically 00 to 59
%M	Minute as two digits, 00 to 59
%H	Hour as per 24-hour clock, 00 to 23
%I	Hour as per 12-hour clock, 01 to 12
%d	Day of the month, 01 to 31
%m	Month (numeric), 01 to 12
%B	Month (string), for example, "October"
%Y	Year as four digits, such as 2016

 For the most complete and up-to-date documentation on displaying time, please refer to the official reference manual—in this case, Python standard library reference, located at https://docs.python.org/.

Binding widgets using properties

Instead of hardcoding an ID for each widget that we need to access from Python code, we can also create a property and assign it in a Kivy language file. The motivation for doing so is mostly the **DRY** principle and cleaner naming, at a cost of a few more lines of code.

Such a property can be defined as follows:

```
# In main.py
from kivy.properties import ObjectProperty
from kivy.uix.boxlayout import BoxLayout

class ClockLayout(BoxLayout):
    time_prop = ObjectProperty(None)
```

In this code fragment, we make a new root widget class for our application based on BoxLayout. It has a custom property, time_prop, which is going to reference Label we need to address from Python code.

Additionally, in the Kivy language file, `clock.kv`, we have to bind this property to a corresponding `id`. Custom properties look and behave no different from the default ones and use exactly the same syntax:

```
ClockLayout:
    time_prop: time

    Label:
        id: time
```

This code makes the `Label` widget accessible from the Python code without knowing the widget's ID, using the newly defined property, `root.time_prop.text = "demo"`.

The described approach is more portable than the previously shown one and it eliminates the need to keep widget identifiers from the Kivy language file in sync with the Python code, for example, when refactoring. Otherwise, the choice between relying on properties and accessing widgets from Python via `root.ids` is a matter of coding style.

Later in this book, we'll explore more advanced usage of Kivy properties, facilitating nearly effortless data binding.

Layout basics

To arrange widgets on the screen, Kivy provides a number of `Layout` classes. `Layout`, a subclass of `Widget`, serves as a container for other widgets. Every layout affects the positioning and size of its children in a unique way.

For this application, we won't need anything fancy, as the desired UI is pretty straightforward. This is what we're aiming to achieve:

A mockup layout of the finished Clock app interface.

To build this, we will use BoxLayout, which is basically a one-dimensional grid. We already have BoxLayout in our clock.kv file, but since it only has one child, it does not affect anything. A rectangular grid with one cell is really just that, a rectangle.

Kivy layouts almost always try to fill the screen, thus our application will adapt to any screen size and orientation changes automatically.

If we add another label to BoxLayout, it will take half the screen space, depending on the orientation: a vertical box layout grows from top to bottom, and horizontal from left to right.

You might have guessed that in order to create a row of buttons inside a vertical layout, we can just embed another, horizontal box layout into the first one. Layouts are widgets, so they can be nested in arbitrary and creative ways to build complex interfaces.

Finalizing the layout

Stacking three widgets into BoxLayout normally makes every widget a third of the available size. Since we don't want buttons to be this big compared to clock displays, we can add a height property to the horizontal (inner) BoxLayout and set its vertical size_hint property to None.

The size_hint property is a tuple of two values, affecting the widget's width and height. We will discuss the impact that size_hint has on different layouts in the next few chapters; right now, let's just say that if we want to use absolute numbers for width or height, we have to set size_hint to None accordingly; otherwise, assigning size won't work as the widget will continue to compute its own size instead of using the values that we'll provide.

After updating the clock.kv file to account for stopwatch display and controls, it should look similar to the following (note the hierarchy of the layouts):

```
BoxLayout:
    orientation: 'vertical'

    Label:
        id: time
        text: '[b]00[/b]:00:00'
        font_name: 'Roboto'
        font_size: 60
        markup: True

    BoxLayout:
```

```
    height: 90
    orientation: 'horizontal'
    padding: 20
    spacing: 20
    size_hint: (1, None)

    Button:
        text: 'Start'
        font_name: 'Roboto'
        font_size: 25
        bold: True

    Button:
        text: 'Reset'
        font_name: 'Roboto'
        font_size: 25
        bold: True

Label:
    id: stopwatch
    text: '00:00.[size=40]00[/size]'
    font_name: 'Roboto'
    font_size: 60
    markup: True
```

If we run the code now, we'll notice that buttons don't fill all the available space inside `BoxLayout`. This effect is achieved using the `padding` and `spacing` properties of the layout. Padding acts very similar to CSS, pushing children (in our case, buttons) away from the edges of the layout, while spacing controls the distance between adjacent children. Both properties default to zero, aiming at maximum widget density.

Reducing repetition

This layout works but has one serious problem: the code is very repetitive. Every change we may want to make has to be done in a number of places throughout the file, and it's very easy to miss one of them and thus introduce an inconsistent change.

To continue the analogy with the web platform, before **CSS**
(**Cascading Style Sheets**) became universally available, style
information was being written directly in tags that surround the text.
It looked like this:

```
<p><font face="Helvetica">Part 1</font></p>
<p><font face="Helvetica">Part 2</font></p>
```

Using this approach, changing any individual element's properties
is easy, but adjusting the properties of the whole document's look
requires an excessive amount of manual labor. If we wanted to
change the font face to Times in the next version of the page, we
would have to search and replace every occurrence of the word
Helvetica while trying to make sure that we don't have this same
word in the running text, as it may be occasionally replaced too.

With style sheets, on the other hand, we move all of the styling
information to a CSS rule:

```
p {font-family: Helvetica}
```

Now we have just one place to account for styling of every paragraph
throughout the document; no more searching and replacing to
change font or any other visual attribute, such as color or padding.
Note that we still may slightly adjust a single element's properties:

```
<p style="font-family: Times">Part 3</p>
```

So we haven't lost anything by implementing CSS, and there is
practically no tradeoff; this explains why the adaptation of style
sheets on the Internet was very fast (especially considering the scale)
and overwhelmingly successful. CSS is being widely used to this day
with no conceptual changes.

In Kivy, there is no need to use a different file for our aggregate styles or class
rules, like it's usually done in web development. We just add to the `clock.kv` file
a definition like the following, outside of `BoxLayout`:

```
<Label>:
    font_name: 'Roboto'
    font_size: 60
    markup: True
```

This is a class rule; it acts similar to a CSS selector described in the previous
information box. Every `Label` derives all the properties from the `<Label>` class rule.
(Note the angle brackets.)

Now we can remove the `font_name`, `font_size`, and `markup` properties from each individual `Label`. As a general rule, always strive to move every repeated definition into a class. This is a well-known best practice called **don't repeat yourself** (**DRY**). Changes like the one shown in the previous code snippet may seem trivial in a toy project like this but will make our code much cleaner and more maintainable in a long run.

If we want to override a property of one of the widgets, just add it as usual. Immediate properties take precedence over those inherited from the class definition.

 Keep in mind that a class definition is completely different from a widget defined in the same `.kv` file. While the syntax is largely the same, the class is just an abstract definition; on its own, it does not create a new widget. Thus, adding a class definition will not introduce any changes to the app if we don't use it later.

Named classes

One obvious problem with the straightforward approach to classes described earlier is that we can only have one class named `Label`. As soon as we need two different sets of properties applied to the same kind of widget, we have to define our own custom classes for them. Additionally, overwriting the framework's built-in classes, such as `Label` or `Button`, may have undesired consequences throughout the application, for example, if another component is using the widget we've altered under the hood.

Fortunately, this is very simple to solve. Let's create a named class for buttons, `RobotoButton`:

```
<RobotoButton@Button>:
    font_name: 'Roboto'
    font_size: 25
    bold: True
```

The part before the `@` symbol designates the new class name, followed by the widget type we're extending (in Python, we would say `class RobotoButton(Button):` instead). The resulting class can be then used in the Kivy language instead of the generic `Button` class:

```
RobotoButton:
    text: 'Start'
```

The use of class rules allows us to reduce the number of recurrent lines in the `clock.kv` file, and also provide a consistent way of tweaking similar widgets using class definitions. Next, let's use this feature to customize all the buttons.

Styling buttons

One of the darker corners of the flat UI paradigm is the look of clickable elements, like that of buttons; there is no universally accepted way of styling them.

For example, the Modern UI style (previously called Metro, as seen in Windows 8) is very radical, with clickable elements that look mostly like flat-colored rectangles with little or no distinctive graphical features. Other vendors, such as Apple, use vibrant gradients; there is a trend of also adding rounded corners, especially in web design since CSS3 provides a special-case syntax for just that. Subtle shadows, while considered heresy by some, aren't unheard of either.

Kivy is flexible in this regard. The framework does not impose any restrictions on visuals and provides a number of useful features to implement any design you like. One of the utilities that we will discuss next is 9-patch image scaling, which is used to style buttons and similar widgets that may have borders.

9-patch scaling

The motivation for a good scaling algorithm is simple: it's almost impossible to provide pixel-perfect graphics for every button, especially for the problematic ones that contain (varying amounts of) text. Scaling images uniformly is simple to implement but yields results that are mediocre at best, partly because of the aspect ratio distortion.

Non-uniform 9-patch scaling, on the other hand, produces uncompromising quality. The idea is to split the image into static and scalable parts. The following image is a hypothetical scalable button. The middle part (shown in yellow) is the working area, and everything else is a border:

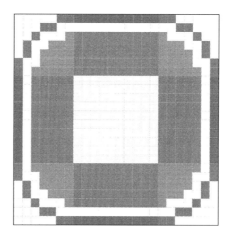

The red zones can be stretched in one dimension, while the blue zones (corners) are always left intact. This is evident from the following screenshot:

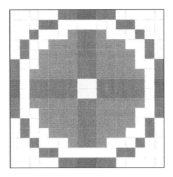

Corners, shown in blue, are fully static and may contain virtually anything. Borders, shown in red, are scalable in one dimension (top and bottom sides can be stretched horizontally, and left and right sides can be stretched vertically). The only part of the image that will be uniformly resized is the inner rectangle, the working area, shown in yellow; it is therefore common to paint it with a flat color. It will also contain text that's assigned to the button, if any.

Using 9-patch images

For this tutorial, we will use a simple flat button with a 1-pixel border. We can reuse this texture for all buttons or choose a different one, for example, for the Reset button. A button texture for the normal state with flat color and 1-pixel border is shown as follows:

The corresponding texture for the pressed state—an inversion of the preceding image—is shown as follows:

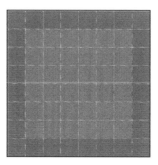

Now, to apply the 9-patch magic, we need to tell Kivy the size of borders that have limited scalability, as discussed previously (the image will be scaled uniformly by default). Let's revisit the `clock.kv` file and add the following properties:

```
<RobotoButton@Button>:
    background_normal: 'button_normal.png'
    background_down: 'button_down.png'
    border: (2, 2, 2, 2)
```

The `border` property values are ordered just like in CSS: top, right, bottom, and left (that is, clockwise starting from the top). Unlike CSS, we can't supply just one value for all sides; at least in the current Kivy version (1.8), the notation `border: 2` results in error.

Probably the shortest way of setting all the borders to the same value is the Python syntax `border: [2] * 4`, which means take a list with a single element, 2, and repeat it four times.

Also note that while the visible border is just one pixel wide, we're assigning the `border` property of customized buttons to 2. This is due to the texture-stretching behavior of the renderer: if pixel colors from both sides of the "cut line" don't match, the result will be a gradient, and we want solid color.

In the class rules overview, we mentioned that the property declared on an instance of a widget takes precedence over the class rule's property with the same name. This can be used to selectively override `background_*`, `border` or any other attribute, for example, assigning another texture while reusing the border width definition:

```
RobotoButton:
    text: 'Reset'
    background_normal: 'red_button_normal.png'
    background_down: 'red_button_down.png'
```

Now our buttons are stylized, but they still don't do anything. The next step towards our goal is making the stopwatch work.

Counting time

Although both stopwatch and the regular clock ultimately just display time, they are completely different in terms of functionality. Wall clock is a strictly increasing monotonic function, while stopwatch time can be paused and reset, decreasing the counter. More practically, the difference is that the operating system readily exposes its internal wall clock to Python, both directly as a `datetime` object and transparently in the case of the `strftime()` function. The latter can be called without a `datetime` argument to format the current time, which is exactly what we need for a wall clock display.

For the task of creating a stopwatch, we will need to build our own, non-monotonic time counter first. This is easily achieved without using Python's time functions altogether, thanks to Kivy's `Clock.schedule_interval` event handler that accepts the time passed between calls as a parameter. This is just what the `nap` parameter does in the following code:

```
def on_start(self):
    Clock.schedule_interval(self.update, 0.016)

def update(self, nap):
    pass
```

Time is measured in seconds, that is, if the app is running at 60 fps and calls our function every frame, the average nap will be $60^{-1} = 0.016(6)$.

With this parameter in place, keeping track of the time passed is simple and can be achieved with a simple increment:

```
class ClockApp(App):
    sw_seconds = 0

    def update(self, nap):
        self.sw_seconds += nap
```

This timer we just created isn't, by definition, a stopwatch since right now, there is no way for the user to actually stop it. However, let's update the display with the incrementing time first so that we can see the effect of controls immediately when implementing them.

Formatting the time for stopwatch

For the main time display, formatting is easy because the standard library function strftime provides us with a number of readily available primitives to convert a datetime object into a readable string representation, according to the provided format string.

This function has a number of limitations:

- It only accepts Python datetime objects (while for the stopwatch, we only have a floating-point number of seconds passed, sw_seconds)
- It has no formatting directive for a decimal fraction of seconds

The former datetime limitation can be easily circumvented: we could cast our sw_seconds variable to datetime. But the latter deficiency makes this unnecessary, as we want to end our notation with fractions of a second (exact to 0.01 sec), so strftime formatting just won't cut it. Hence, we implement our own time formatting.

Computing values

First, we need to compute the necessary values: minutes, seconds, and fractions of a second. The math is easy; here's the one-liner for minutes and seconds:

```
minutes, seconds = divmod(self.sw_seconds, 60)
```

Note the use of the divmod function. This is a shorthand for the following:

```
minutes = self.sw_seconds / 60
seconds = self.sw_seconds % 60
```

While being more concise, the divmod version should also perform better on most Python interpreters, as it performs the division just once. On today's machines, the floating-point division is quite effective, but if we run a whole lot of such operations every frame, like in a video game or simulation, the CPU time will quickly add up.

 Generally, the author tends to disagree with the oft-chanted mantra about premature optimization being evil; many bad practices that lead to choppy and substandard performance can and should be easily avoided without compromising on code quality, and not doing so is by all means premature pessimization.

Also note that both minutes and seconds values are still floating-point, so we will need to convert them to integers before we print them: int(minutes) and int(seconds).

Now all that's left is hundredths of seconds; we can compute them like this:

```
int(seconds * 100 % 100)
```

Putting a stopwatch in place

We have all the values; let's join them together. Formatting strings in Python is quite a common task, and contrary to The Zen of Python commandment that reads, "There should be one—and preferably only one—obvious way to do it" (`https://www.python.org/dev/peps/pep-0020/`), there are several common idioms for string formatting. We will use one of the simplest, operator %, which is somewhat similar to the `sprintf()` function commonly found in other programming languages:

```
def update_time(self, nap):
    self.sw_seconds += nap
    minutes, seconds = divmod(self.sw_seconds, 60)
    self.root.ids.stopwatch.text = (
        '%02d:%02d.[size=40]%02d[/size]' %
        (int(minutes), int(seconds),
         int(seconds * 100 % 100)))
```

Since we have fractions of a second now, the refresh frequency of 1 fps that we used earlier isn't sufficient anymore. Let's set it to 0 instead so that our `update_time` function will be called for every frame:

```
Clock.schedule_interval(self.update_time, 0)
```

Today, most displays run at a refresh rate of 60 fps, while our value is exact to 1/100 sec, that is, changes 100 times per second. While we could have attempted to run our function at exactly 100 fps, there is absolutely no reason to do it: for users, it isn't possible to see the difference on commonly available hardware, as the display will still update no more than 60 times per second anyway.

That said, most of the time your code should work independently of a frame rate, as it relies on the user's hardware, and there is no way to predict what machine your application will end up on. Even today's smartphones have wildly different system specs and performance, let alone laptops and desktop computers.

And that's it; if we run the application now, we'll see an incrementing counter. It lacks interactivity yet, and this will be our next target.

Stopwatch controls

Controlling the application by the means of button press events is very easy. All that we need to do for this to work is use the following code:

```
def start_stop(self):
    self.root.ids.start_stop.text = ('Start'
        if self.sw_started else 'Stop')
    self.sw_started = not self.sw_started

def reset(self):
    if self.sw_started:
        self.root.ids.start_stop.text = 'Start'
        self.sw_started = False
    self.sw_seconds = 0
```

The first event handler is for the **Start** and **Stop** buttons. It changes the state (`sw_started`) and the button caption. The second handler reverts everything to the initial state.

We also need to add the state property to keep track of whether the stopwatch is running or paused:

```
class ClockApp(App):
    sw_started = False
    sw_seconds = 0

    def update_clock(self, nap):
        if self.sw_started:
            self.sw_seconds += nap
```

We change the `update_clock` function so that it increments `sw_seconds` only if the stopwatch is started, that is, `sw_started` is set to `True`. Initially, the stopwatch isn't started.

In the `clock.kv` file, we bind these new methods to `on_press` events:

```
RobotoButton:
    id: start_stop
    text: 'Start'
    on_press: app.start_stop()

RobotoButton:
    id: reset
    text: 'Reset'
    on_press: app.reset()
```

In Kivy language, we have several context-sensitive references at our disposal. They are as follows:

- `self`: This always refers to the current widget;
- `root`: This is the outermost widget of a given scope;
- `app`: This is the application class instance.

As you can see, implementing event handling for buttons isn't hard at all. At this point, our app provides interaction with the stopwatch, allowing the user to start, stop, and reset it. For the purposes of this tutorial, we're done.

Summary

In this chapter, we built a functional Kivy app, ready to be deployed to, for example, Google Play or another app store for public use. This requires a bit of extra work and the process of packaging is platform-specific, but the hardest part—programming—is over.

With the Clock app, we managed to showcase many areas of the Kivy application's development cycle without making the code unnecessarily lengthy or convoluted. Keeping the code short and concise is a major feature of the framework because it allows us to experiment and iterate quickly. Being able to implement new bits of functionality with very little old code getting in the way is invaluable. Kivy surely lives up to its description as a library for rapid application development.

One general principle that we will encounter throughout the book (and Kivy development at large) is that neither our program nor Kivy exist in the void; we always have the whole platform at our disposal, consisting of a rich Python standard library, a lot of other libraries available from the Python *cheese shop*—the **Python Package Index (PyPI)** located at `http://pypi.python.org`—and elsewhere, and the underlying operating system services.

We can also retool many web-development-oriented assets easily, reusing fonts, colors, and shapes from CSS frameworks, such as Bootstrap. And by all means take a look at Google's *Material design principles*—this isn't just a collection of design assets, but a complete field guide that allows us to achieve a consistent and good-looking UI without sacrificing the identity or "personality" of our application.

This is, of course, only the beginning. Many features that were briefly discussed in this chapter will be explored more in-depth later in this book.

2
Building a Paint App

In *Chapter 1*, *Building a Clock App*, we built an application from Kivy's standard components: layouts, text labels, and buttons. We were able to significantly customize the look of these components while retaining a very high level of abstraction—working with full-fledged widgets, as opposed to individual graphical primitives. This is convenient for certain types of applications but not always desirable, and as you will see shortly, the Kivy framework also provides tools to work with a lower level of abstraction: draw points and lines.

I believe that the best way to play with free-form graphics is by building a painting app. Our application, when complete, will be somewhat similar to the MS Paint application that comes bundled with the Windows OS.

Unlike Microsoft Paint, our Kivy Paint app will be fully cross-platform, including mobile devices running Android and iOS. Also, we will deliberately omit many features found in "real" software for image processing, such as rectangular selection, layers, and saving files to disk. Implementing them can be a good exercise for you.

Regarding mobile devices: while building a fully functional iOS application with Kivy is of course possible, it's still non-trivial if you have no experience with either iOS or Kivy development. Therefore, it's recommended that you write for easy platforms first so that you can quickly update your code and run the application without building binaries and such. In this sense, Android development is much simpler, thanks to Kivy Launcher, a generic environment to run Kivy apps on Android. It is available on Google Play at `https://play.google.com/store/apps/details?id=org.kivy.pygame`.

The ability to immediately launch and test your app without compiling is an incredibly important aspect of Kivy development. This allows programmers to iterate quickly and evaluate possible solutions on the spot, which is crucial for **rapid application development (RAD)** and the agile methodology as a whole.

With the notable exception of window resizing, which isn't widely used on mobiles, Kivy apps behave in a similar way on various mobile and desktop platforms. So it's perfectly feasible to write and debug just the desktop or Android version of the program until much later in the release cycle and then fill the compatibility gaps, if any.

We will also explore two distinctive, almost mutually exclusive features available to Kivy apps: multitouch controls, useful on devices with a touch screen, and changing mouse pointers on a desktop computer.

Staying true to its mobile-first approach, Kivy provides an emulation layer for multitouch input, usable with the mouse. It can be triggered with a right-click. This multitouch emulation isn't, however, suitable for any real-world usage, except for debugging; it will be turned off in the production version of the application when running on a desktop.

This is what our application will look like at the end of the chapter:

The Kivy Paint app, bad painting sold separately

Setting the stage

Initially, the entire surface of our app is occupied by the **root widget**, in this case, that's the canvas the user can paint upon. We won't devote any screen space to the instruments' area until later.

As you probably know by now, the root widget is the outermost widget in the hierarchy. Every Kivy application has one, and it can be pretty much anything, depending on the desired behavior. As seen in *Chapter 1*, *Building a Clock App*, BoxLayout is a suitable root widget; it was sufficient as we had no additional requirements for it, and layouts are designed to work as containers for other controls.

In the case of a Paint app, we need its root widget to adhere to much more interesting requirements; the user should be able to draw lines, possibly utilizing multitouch functionality, if available. At the moment, Kivy has no built-in controls suitable for the task at hand, so we will need to create our own.

Building new Kivy widgets is simple. As soon as our class inherits from Kivy's
`Widget` class, we're good to go. So the simplest custom widget that does nothing
special, together with the Kivy application that uses it, can be implemented like this:

```
from kivy.app import App
from kivy.uix.widget import Widget

class CanvasWidget(Widget):
    pass

class PaintApp(App):
    def build(self):
        return CanvasWidget()

if __name__ == '__main__':
    PaintApp().run()
```

This is the full listing of our Paint app's starting point, `main.py`, complete with the
`PaintApp` class. In future chapters, we will omit simple boilerplate like this; this one
is provided for the sake of completeness.

 The `Widget` class usually serves as a base class, like `object`
in Python or `Object` Java. While it's possible to use it "as is"
in the application, `Widget` itself is of very limited utility. It
has no visual appearance and no properties that would be
immediately useful in the program. Subclassing `Widget`, on
the other hand, is pretty straightforward and useful in many
different scenarios.

Fine-tuning the looks

First, let's tweak the appearance of our app. This isn't exactly a critical functionality,
but bear with me here, as these customizations are commonly requested and also
pretty easy to set up. I'll briefly describe the properties that we covered in the
previous chapter, and we'll add a number of new tweaks, such as window size and
change of the mouse cursor.

Visual appearance

I strongly believe that the background color of any Paint app should initially be white. You're probably already familiar with this setting from the first chapter. Here's the line of code we add after the __name__ == '__main__' line to achieve the desired effect:

```
from kivy.core.window import Window
from kivy.utils import get_color_from_hex

Window.clearcolor = get_color_from_hex('#FFFFFF')
```

You may want to put most of the import lines where they usually belong, near the beginning of a program file. As you will learn shortly, some imports in Kivy are actually order-dependent and have side effects, most notably the Window object. This is rarely the case in well-behaved Python programs, and the side effects of the import statement are generally considered bad application design.

Window size

Another commonly tweaked property of a desktop application is window size. The following changes will have absolutely no effect on mobile devices.

It's also worth noting that by default, Kivy's window on a desktop can be resized by the end user. We will learn how to disable that shortly (only for the sake of completeness; usually, that's not such a great idea).

 Setting the window size programmatically is also a handy thing to do when you're targeting a mobile device whose specifications are known in advance. This allows you to test the application on a desktop using the correct screen resolution of the target device.

To assign the initial window size, insert the next code snippet right above the line that reads from kivy.core.window import Window. It's critical to apply these settings before the Window object is even imported; otherwise, they won't have any effect:

```
from kivy.config import Config

Config.set('graphics', 'width', '960')
Config.set('graphics', 'height', '540')  # 16:9
```

In addition, you may want to disable window resizing by adding this one line:

```
Config.set('graphics', 'resizable', '0')
```

Please don't do this unless you have a very good reason, since taking these trivial customizations away from the user is usually a bad idea and can easily ruin the overall user experience. Building a pixel-perfect app in just one resolution is tempting, but many of your customers (especially mobile users) won't be happy. Kivy layouts, on the other hand, make building scalable interfaces bearable.

Mouse cursor

The next customization that generally applies only to desktop apps is changing the mouse pointer. Kivy has no abstraction for this, so we will work at a lower level, importing and calling methods directly from Pygame, the SDL-based window and OpenGL context provider, which is commonly used by Kivy on desktop platforms.

This code, if you choose to implement it, should always be run conditionally. Most mobile and some desktop apps won't have a Pygame window, and we surely want to avoid crashing the program over a trivial and non-essential matter like the mouse cursor.

Long story short, this is the mouse pointer format that's used by Pygame:

```
CURSOR = (
    '                 @@@@                ',
    '                 @--@                ',
    '                 @--@                ',
    '                 @--@                ',
    '                 @--@                ',
    '                 @@@@                ',
    '                                     ',
    '@@@@@@ @@@@ @@@@@@                    ',
    '@----@ @--@ @----@                   ',
    '@----@ @--@ @----@                   ',
    '@@@@@@ @@@@ @@@@@@                    ',
    '                                     ',
    '                 @@@@                ',
    '                 @--@                ',
    '                 @--@                ',
    '                 @--@                ',
    '                 @--@                ',
    '                 @@@@                ',
    '                                     ',
    '                                     ',
    '                                     ',
    '                                     ',
    '                                     ',
    '                                     ',
)
```

The ASCII format used to describe a custom mouse pointer

Every character in this notation stands for one pixel: '@' is black and '-' is white; everything else is transparent. All lines have to be of equal width, divisible by eight (a restriction imposed by the underlying SDL implementation).

When used in an application, it should look as depicted in the next screenshot (the image is significantly zoomed in, obviously):

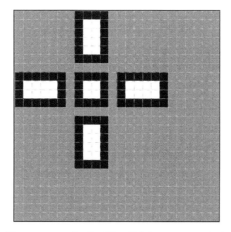

Mouse cursor for the Kivy Paint app: a crosshair

There is a caveat though. At the time of writing this, the version of Pygame that's commonly available in some operating systems has a bug in the pygame.cursors.compile() function that switches between white and black. Detecting the affected versions of Pygame is impractical, so we'll just include the correctly working function in our code and won't call the potentially buggy version of the same function.

The correct function, pygame_compile_cursor(), that translates the Pygame's mouse cursor definition into something expected by **Simple DirectMedia Layer (SDL)**, Pygame's backend library, is available online at http://goo.gl/2KaepD.

Now, to actually apply the resulting cursor to the application window, we'll replace our PaintApp.build method with the following:

```
from kivy.base import EventLoop
class PaintApp(App):
    def build(self):
        EventLoop.ensure_window()
        if EventLoop.window.__class__.__name__.endswith('Pygame'):
```

```
try:
    from pygame import mouse
    # pygame_compile_cursor is a fixed version of
    # pygame.cursors.compile
    a, b = pygame_compile_cursor()
    mouse.set_cursor((24, 24), (9, 9), a, b)
except:
    pass


return CanvasWidget()
```

The code is pretty straightforward, but some aspects of it may need explanation. Here is a quick walk-through:

- `EventLoop.ensure_window()`: This function call blocks the execution until we have the application window (`EventLoop.window`) ready.

- `if EventLoop.window.__class__.__name__.endswith('Pygame'):` This condition checks the window class name (not the greatest way to make assertions about the code, but works in this case). We want to run our mouse cursor customization code only for a certain window provider, in this case, Pygame.

- The remaining part of the code, enclosed in a `try ... except` block, is a Pygame-specific `mouse.set_cursor` call.

- Variables `a` and `b` constitute the internal representation of the cursor used by SDL, namely the XOR and AND mask. They are binary and should be considered an opaque implementation detail of the SDL.

 As usual, please refer to the official reference manual for the full API specification. Pygame documentation can be found at `http://www.pygame.org`.

This entire situation when we're working at a level of abstraction much lower than Kivy's isn't very common, but by all means, don't be afraid to dive into implementation details sometimes. There are many things that can be achieved only in the underlying library because Kivy does not provide meaningful abstractions for them. This especially applies to non-cross-platform functionality, such as OS-dependent app interoperability, notification services, and so on.

To reiterate, this diagram summarizes the abstraction levels we traverse in this specific case to set the mouse pointer:

Kivy			
Uses Pygame to control window lifecycle. Has no concept of mouse cursor.	**Pygame** Provides a Python API to SDL. Can control mouse cursor.	**SDL** This is a unified API on top of different operating systems.	**OS** Provides low-level API to practically everything.

The relationship of Kivy, Pygame, SDL, and the underlying operating system abstractions

Thankfully, we didn't have to work directly with the operating system—cross-platform functionality can be surprisingly hard to get right. This is exactly what SDL does.

> While we don't work with the SDL directly, you might still want to take a look at the documentation found at `https://www.libsdl.org/`—this will give you a perspective on the underlying low-level API calls that Kivy ultimately relies on.

Multitouch emulation

By default, Kivy provides an emulation mode for multitouch operations when running on a desktop system. It is activated with a right-click and spawns permanent touches rendered as semi-transparent red dots; they can also be dragged while holding the right mouse button.

This feature may be nice for debugging, especially when you don't have a real multitouch device to test on; users, on the other hand, won't be expecting this functionality bound to the right click. It's probably a good idea to disable it so that our users don't get confused by this not very useful or obvious emulation mode. For this, add the following to the initialization sequence:

```
Config.set('input', 'mouse', 'mouse,disable_multitouch')
```

This code can be made conditional (or just commented out temporarily) at the time of development if you're actually using this feature for debugging.

Drawing touches

To illustrate one possible scenario for reacting to the touch input, let's draw a circle every time the user touches (or clicks) the screen.

A `Widget` has an `on_touch_down` event that will come in handy for this task. We're interested in just the coordinates of every touch for the time being, and they are accessible as follows:

```
class CanvasWidget(Widget):
    def on_touch_down(self, touch):
        print(touch.x, touch.y)
```

This example prints the position of touches as they occur. To draw something on the screen instead, we will use the `Widget.canvas` property. Kivy's `Canvas` is a logical drawable surface that abstracts away the underlying OpenGL renderer. Unlike the low-level graphical API, the canvas is stateful and preserves the drawing instructions that were added to it.

Speaking of drawing primitives, many of those can be imported from the `kivy.graphics` package. Examples of drawing instructions are `Color`, `Line`, `Rectangle`, and `Bezier`, among others.

A very short introduction to the canvas

The `Canvas` API can be invoked directly or as a context handler using the `with` keyword. A simple (direct) invocation looks like this:

```
self.canvas.add(Line(circle=(touch.x, touch.y, 25)))
```

This adds a `Line` primitive with arguments to a graphical instructions queue.

> If you want to try out this code right off the bat, please see the next section, *Displaying touches on the screen*, for a more comprehensive example of using canvas instructions in the context of our Paint app.

Using the context handler generally looks nicer and less cluttered, especially when applying multiple instructions. It is shown in the following example, which is functionally equivalent to the previous code snippet with `self.canvas.add()`:

```
with self.canvas:
    Line(circle=(touch.x, touch.y, 25))
```

This may seem a bit harder to grasp than the direct approach. Choosing the code style to use is a matter of personal preference, as they achieve the same thing.

Note that, as mentioned before, every subsequent call gets added to the canvas without affecting the instructions that were applied previously; at the core, the canvas is a growing array of instructions that are replayed every time the surface is rendered to the screen. Keep this in mind: as we aim for 60 fps refresh rate, we certainly don't want this list to grow indefinitely.

For example, one of the coding practices that works correctly on the immediate-mode-rendering surface (like HTML5's <canvas>) is erasing the previously drawn graphics from the view by overpainting it with background color. This is rather intuitive and works correctly in a browser:

```
// JavaScript code for clearing the canvas
canvas.rect(0, 0, width, height)
canvas.fillStyle = '#FFFFFF'
canvas.fill()
```

In Kivy, on the other hand, this pattern still just adds drawing instructions; it first renders all of the pre-existing primitives and then paints them over with a rectangle. This looks just about right (the canvas is visually empty) but does the wrong thing:

```
# Same code as JavaScript above. This is wrong, don't do it!
with self.canvas:
    Color(1, 1, 1)
    Rectangle(pos=self.pos, size=self.size)
```

> Just like a memory leak, this bug can go unnoticed for a long time, quietly accumulating rendering instructions and degrading performance. Thanks to powerful video cards found in today's devices, including smartphones, rendering is generally very fast. So it's hard to realize that the overhead is there when debugging.
>
> In order to properly clear the canvas in Kivy (that is, remove all the drawing instructions), you should use the canvas.clear() method, shown later in this chapter.

Displaying touches on the screen

We are going to implement a button to clear the screen shortly; in the meantime, let's display touches on the screen. We remove the call to print() and add the following method to the CanvasWidget class definition:

```
class CanvasWidget(Widget):
    def on_touch_down(self, touch):
        with self.canvas:
            Color(*get_color_from_hex('#0080FF80'))
            Line(circle=(touch.x, touch.y, 25), width=4)
```

This draws an empty circle around every touch that our widget receives. The `Color` instruction sets the color for the following `Line` primitive.

> Note that the color format (here, #RRGGBBAA) isn't strictly CSS conformant, as it has the fourth component, namely the alpha channel (transparency). This syntax variation should be self-evident. It's akin to, for example, `rgb()` and `rgba()` notations commonly found elsewhere.

You may have also noticed how we're using `Line` in quite an unorthodox way here, drawing circles instead of straight lines. Many Kivy graphical primitives are powerful like that. For example, any canvas instruction, such as the `Rectangle` or `Triangle` primitive, can render a background image, given a `source` parameter.

If you're following along, this is how the result should look so far:

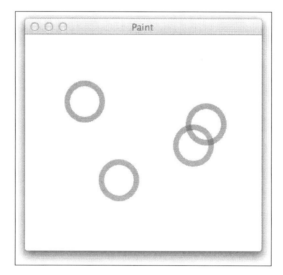

Displaying touches on the screen

The full source code up to this point, which was used to produce the preceding demonstration, reads:

```python
# In main.py
from kivy.app import App
from kivy.config import Config
from kivy.graphics import Color, Line
from kivy.uix.widget import Widget
from kivy.utils import get_color_from_hex

class CanvasWidget(Widget):
```

```
    def on_touch_down(self, touch):
        with self.canvas:
            Color(*get_color_from_hex('#0080FF80'))
            Line(circle=(touch.x, touch.y, 25), width=4)

class PaintApp(App):
    def build(self):
        return CanvasWidget()


if __name__ == '__main__':
    Config.set('graphics', 'width', '400')
    Config.set('graphics', 'height', '400')
    Config.set('input', 'mouse',
               'mouse,disable_multitouch')

    from kivy.core.window import Window
    Window.clearcolor = get_color_from_hex('#FFFFFF')

    PaintApp().run()
```

This excludes the nonessential mouse cursor part for the sake of keeping the example code short and sweet. The accompanying Kivy language file, `paint.kv`, is missing altogether at this point—instead, the `build()` method of the app class returns the root widget.

Observe the unusual placement of the `import Window` line. This is due to the side effects of this specific module, already mentioned earlier. `Config.set()` calls should precede this `import` statement to have any effect.

Next, we are going to add more features to our little program, bringing it in line with the desired Paint app behavior.

Clearing the screen

Right now, the only way to clear the screen in our little app is to restart it. Let's add a button for deleting everything from the canvas to our UI, which is very minimalistic at the moment. We'll reuse the button look from the previous app, so there will be nothing new about theming; the interesting part here is positioning.

In our first program, the Clock app from *Chapter 1, Building a Clock App*, we didn't work on any explicit positioning at all, as everything was being held in place by nested `BoxLayout`s. Now, however, we don't have any layout to our program as the root widget is our very own `CanvasWidget`, and we didn't implement any logic to position its children.

In Kivy, the absence of an explicit layout means that every widget has full control over its placement and size (this is pretty much the default state of affairs in many other UI toolkits, such as Delphi, Visual Basic, and so on).

To position the newly created delete button in the top-right corner, we do the following:

```
# In paint.kv
<CanvasWidget>:
    Button:
        text: 'Delete'
        right: root.right
        top: root.top
        width: 80
        height: 40
```

This is a property binding that says the button's `right` and `top` properties should be kept in sync with the root widget's properties accordingly. We could also do the math here, for example, `root.top - 20`. The rest is pretty straightforward, as `width` and `height` are absolute values.

Also note that we've defined a class rule for `<CanvasWidget>` without specifying its superclass. This works because this time we are extending the existing class with the same name, defined earlier in Python code. Kivy allows us to augment all the existing widget classes, both built-ins, such as `<Button>` and `<Label>`, and custom ones.

This illustrates a common good practice to describe visual attributes of objects using the Kivy language. At the same time, it's better to keep all program flow constructs, such as event handlers, on the Python side of things. Such separation of concerns makes both the Python source code and its corresponding Kivy language counterpart more readable and easier to follow.

Passing events

If you have kept up with this tutorial and already tried clicking the button, you may have noticed (or even guessed) that it doesn't work. The fact that it doesn't do anything useful is obviously due to the missing click handler that we're going to implement shortly. What's more interesting is that the click just doesn't get through, as there is no visual feedback; instead, the usual semi-transparent circle gets painted on top of the button, and that's it.

This strange effect happens because we're processing all the touches in the `CanvasWidget.on_touch_down` handler and don't pass them to the children, so they cannot react. Unlike HTML's **Document Object Model (DOM)**, events in Kivy don't bubble up from the nested element up to its parent. They go the other way around, from the parent down to the children, that is, if the parent widget would pass them, which it doesn't.

This could be fixed by explicitly doing something along the lines of the following code:

```
# Caution: suboptimal approach!
def on_touch_down(self, touch):
    for widget in self.children:
        widget.on_touch_down(touch)
```

In reality, that's pretty much what the default behavior (`Widget.on_touch_down`) already does, so we may as well call it and make the code much more concise, as follows:

```
def on_touch_down(self, touch):
    if Widget.on_touch_down(self, touch):
        return
```

The default `on_touch_down` handler also returns `True` if the event was actually processed in a meaningful way. Touching a button will return `True` since the button reacts to it, and at the very least, changes its appearance. That's just what we need in order to cancel our own event processing, which amounts to drawing circles at this time, hence the `return` statement on the second line of the method.

Clearing the canvas

Now we move on to the easiest and also the most useful part of the **Delete** button—a touch handler that erases everything. Clearing the canvas is quite simple, so everything we need to do in order to get this function to work is here. Yup, just two lines of code grand total:

```
def clear_canvas(self):
    self.canvas.clear()
```

Don't forget to add this method as an event handler to the `paint.kv` file:

```
Button:
    on_release: root.clear_canvas()
```

It works, except that it also removes the **Delete** button itself! This happens because the button is a child of `CanvasWidget` (naturally, since `CanvasWidget` is a root widget, everything is its direct or indirect child). And while the button widget itself isn't deleted (and clicking it still clears the screen), its canvas (`Button.canvas`) gets removed from the `CanvasWidget.canvas.children` hierarchy and is thus no longer rendered.

The very straightforward way of fixing it is like this:

```
def clear_canvas(self):
    self.canvas.clear()
    self.canvas.children = [widget.canvas
                            for widget in self.children]
```

However, this isn't nice because widgets may do their own initialization and arrange things differently. A better way to solve this issue is to do the following:

1. Remove all the children from the "offending" widget (`CanvasWidget`, in this case).

2. Clear the canvas.

3. Finally, re-add child widgets back so that they can initialize their rendering properly.

The revised version of the code is a bit longer but works properly and is more bulletproof:

```
class CanvasWidget(Widget):
    def clear_canvas(self):
        saved = self.children[:]  # See below
        self.clear_widgets()
        self.canvas.clear()
        for widget in saved:
            self.add_widget(widget)
```

One line that may need explanation is the `saved = self.children[:]` expression. The `[:]` operation is an array copy (literally, "create a new array with these same elements"). If we write `saved = self.children` instead, this means we're copying a pointer to an array; later, when we call `self.clear_widgets()`, it will remove everything from both `self.children` and `saved` since they're referring to the same object in the memory. This is why `self.children[:]` is required. (The behavior we just discussed is how Python works and is not related to Kivy.)

If you're not familiar with the slicing syntax in Python, please see the StackOverflow thread at `http://stackoverflow.com/questions/509211` for an example.

At this stage, we can already kind of paint things with blue bubbles, as depicted in the following screenshot. This is clearly not the final behavior of our Paint app, so please read on to the next section in which we will make it draw actual lines.

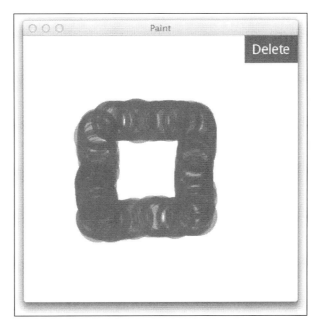

The Delete button in all its dreadful glory. Also, painting with a circle "brush"

Connecting the dots

Our app already has a clear screen function but still draws just circles. Let's change it so that we can draw lines instead.

To follow continuous touch events (click-and-drag), we'll need to add a new event listener, `on_touch_move`. Every time the callback is invoked, it receives the latest point where the event occurred.

If we only had a single line going at every moment (like typically done on a desktop, since there is only one mouse pointer anyway), we could save the line we're currently drawing in `self.current_line`. But since we're aiming at multitouch support from the very beginning, we'll take another approach and store every line being drawn in the corresponding `touch` variable itself.

This works because for every continuous touch from start to end, all callbacks receive the same `touch` object. There is also a `touch.ud` property of the type `dict` (where `ud` is short for user data), which is specifically tailored to keep touch-specific attributes between event handler invocations. Initially, the `touch.ud` property is an empty Python dictionary, `{}`.

What we're going to do next is:

- In the `on_touch_down` handler, create a new line and store it in the `touch.ud` dictionary. This time, we will use regular straight lines instead of the fancy circular lines we employed earlier to illustrate where individual touches would land.

- In `on_touch_move`, append a new point to the end of the corresponding line. We are adding a straight line segment, but since the event handler is going to be invoked many times per second, the end result will consist of a series of very short segments and will look rather smooth nevertheless.

 More advanced graphical programs are using sophisticated algorithms to make lines appear as if they were drawn on a real physical surface. This includes using Bezier curves to make lines seamless even at high resolution and extrapolating line thickness from the pointer movement's speed or pressure. We aren't going to implement these here as they bear no relation to Kivy, but adding these techniques to the resulting Paint app may constitute a nice exercise for the reader.

The code, as we just described, is listed as follows:

```
from kivy.graphics import Color, Line

class CanvasWidget(Widget):
    def on_touch_down(self, touch):
        if Widget.on_touch_down(self, touch):
            return

        with self.canvas:
            Color(*get_color_from_hex('#0080FF80'))
            touch.ud['current_line'] = Line(
                points=(touch.x, touch.y), width=2)

    def on_touch_move(self, touch):
        if 'current_line' in touch.ud:
            touch.ud['current_line'].points += (touch.x, touch.y)
```

This simple approach works, and we're able to draw boring blue lines on our canvas. Now let's give our users the ability to select color, then we'll be one step closer to a painting app that's actually somewhat useful.

The color palette

Every painting program comes with a palette to choose colors from, and ours will be no exception by the time we reach the end of this section, real soon.

Conceptually, a palette is just a list of available colors, presented in a way that makes choosing the right color easy. In a full-fledged image editor, it usually includes every color available on the system (commonly a full 24-bit true color or the 16,777,216 unique colors). The customary representation of this all-encompassing palette typically looks like the following:

Illustration of a true color palette window

On the other hand, if we aren't going to compete with popular proprietary image editing applications, we might as well ship a limited selection of colors. For a person with little to no background in graphics, this may even pose a competitive advantage—choosing fitting colors that look good together is hard. For this exact reason, there are palettes on the Internet that may be universally used for UI and graphic design.

In this tutorial, we are going to make use of the Flat UI style guide (available at http://designmodo.github.io/Flat-UI/), which is based on a list of carefully chosen colors that work great together. Alternatively, feel free to choose any other palette you like, which is purely an aesthetic preference.

There is much to learn in the area of colors, especially color compatibility and suitability for specific tasks. Low-contrast combinations may work great for decorative elements or big headlines, but they fall short for the main article's text; however, counterintuitively, very high contrast, like white on black, is not easy on the eyes and quickly strains them.

So, a good rule of thumb regarding colors is that unless you are absolutely confident in your artistic skills, preferably stick to well-established palettes that are successfully used by others. A great place to start is your favorite operating system's or desktop environment's guidelines. The following are some of the examples:

- Tango palette, which is widely used in open source environments such as desktop Linux, can be found at `http://tango.freedesktop.org/Tango_Icon_Theme_Guidelines`.
- Google Material design principles, presented at the Google I/O conference in 2014, is available at `https://www.google.com/design/material-design.pdf`.
- The unofficial iOS 7 color swatches can be found at `http://ios7colors.com/` (many people, including me, find these a bit exaggerated and too vibrant, thus best suited for games and maybe advertising, as opposed to a UI for daily use).

There are many more color palettes for various tasks readily available — check Google if interested, or use a color picker on your favorite OS and programs.

Subclassing the buttons

Since we're going for a rather short fixed list of colors, the UI controls that are best suited to represent such a list are likely toggle or radio buttons. Kivy's `ToggleButton` would be perfectly suitable for this task, but it has an unfortunate limitation: in a toggle group, all buttons may be deselected at once. This would mean that, in the context of the Paint app, there is no color selected. (One possible option in this case is to fall back to a default color, but this may be surprising to the user so we won't take this approach.)

The good news is that with Python's **OOP (object-oriented programming)** capabilities, we can easily subclass `ToggleButton` and alter its behavior to do what we need, that is, to forbid the deselection of the currently selected button. After this tweak, exactly one color will be selected at all times.

Subclassing will also achieve another goal in this case: for a palette, we want to paint every button in its distinctive color. While we could certainly employ the previously used technique of assigning background images to buttons, this would require us to produce a whole lot of different background images. Instead, we are going to use the background color property, which can be assigned from the paint.kv file.

This architecture allows us to keep the definition of the palette itself in a very readable declarative form inside paint.kv, while the implementation details stay out of our way in a subclass—exactly how an OOP program should be.

Taking away the ability to deselect

First, let's make toggle buttons that cannot all be deselected simultaneously.

To illustrate the problem (and also create the bare-bones implementation that will serve as a starting point), let's implement the desired UI using standard Kivy's ToggleButton widgets. This part is purely declarative; let's just add the following code to paint.kv to the bottom of the <CanvasWidget> section:

```
BoxLayout:
    orientation: 'horizontal'
    padding: 3
    spacing: 3
    x: 0
    y: 0
    width: root.width
    height: 40

    ToggleButton:
        group: 'color'
        text: 'Red'

    ToggleButton:
        group: 'color'
        text: 'Blue'
        state: 'down'
```

We use the familiar BoxLayout component here, acting as a toolbar for individual color buttons. The layout widget itself is positioned absolutely, with x and y both set to 0 (that is, the bottom-left corner), taking the full width of CanvasWidget.

Each ToggleButton belongs to the same group, 'color', so that at most only one of these can be selected (state: 'down') at the same time.

Overriding the standard behavior

As mentioned previously, the built-in `ToggleButton` behavior isn't exactly the radio button that we need; if you click on the selected button, it will be deselected, leaving the whole toggle group without a selected element.

To fix it, let's subclass `ToggleButton` as follows:

```
from kivy.uix.behaviors import ToggleButtonBehavior
from kivy.uix.togglebutton import ToggleButton

class RadioButton(ToggleButton):
    def _do_press(self):
        if self.state == 'normal':
            ToggleButtonBehavior._do_press(self)
```

That's it. We allow the button to toggle like it normally would only if it wasn't already selected (its `state` is `'normal'`, as opposed to `'down'`).

Now all that's left is to replace every instance of `ToggleButton` in the `paint.kv` file with `RadioButton`, the name of our custom class, and instantly see the difference in the behavior of buttons.

This is a major selling point of the Kivy framework: in only a few lines, you can override the built-in functions and methods, achieving practically unmatched flexibility.

> To become usable in Kivy language, the `RadioButton` definition should reside in the `main.py` module or be imported into its scope. Since we have just one Python file now, that's a non-issue, but as your application grows, do keep this in mind: custom Kivy widgets, like other Python classes or functions, have to be imported prior to their first use.

Coloring buttons

Now that our buttons behave properly, the next step is coloring. What we're aiming for will look like the following image:

Paint app's color palette, vibrant and inviting

To achieve this, we are going to use the `background_color` property. The background color in Kivy acts as a tint and not just a solid color; we need to prepare a pure white background image first, which, when tinted, will give us the color we want. This way, we only need to prepare two button textures (normal and pressed state) for any number of arbitrary colored buttons.

The images we use here aren't very different from those we prepared previously for the Clock app in *Chapter 1, Building a Clock App*, except that now the main area of a button is white to allow coloring, and the selected state features a black border:

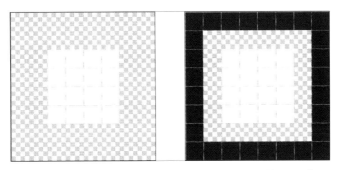

The color button's texture, where the white area will be tinted
using the background color property

A new kind of button

This time, we can do most of the work, including creating a new button class, in the `paint.kv` file. The new class will be called `ColorButton`:

```
<ColorButton@RadioButton>:
    group: 'color'
    on_release: app.canvas_widget.set_color(self.background_color)
    background_normal: 'color_button_normal.png'
    background_down: 'color_button_down.png'
    border: (3, 3, 3, 3)
```

As you can see, we've moved the `group` property here to avoid cluttering the palette definition with repetitive `group: 'color'` lines.

We're also assigning an event handler, `on_release`, that will be called when a `ColorButton` is pressed. Every button passes its `background_color` property to the event handler, so all that's left to do is assign this color to the canvas. This event will be handled by `CanvasWidget`, which needs to be exposed from the `PaintApp` class, as follows:

```
class PaintApp(App):
    def build(self):
```

```
# The set_color() method will be implemented shortly.
self.canvas_widget = CanvasWidget()
self.canvas_widget.set_color(
    get_color_from_hex('#2980B9'))
return self.canvas_widget
```

The reason for this arrangement is that we cannot use the `root` shortcut in the preceding `paint.kv` class definition; it will point at the `ColorButton` itself (the root definition inside the class rule is indeed the class rule itself because it's defined at the top level in `paint.kv`). We can also set the default color here, as shown in the code snippet.

While we're in the `main.py` module, let's also implement the `set_color()` method on `CanvasWidget`, which will serve as an event handler for `ColorButton` clicks. The method in question is very straightforward:

```
def set_color(self, new_color):
    self.canvas.add(Color(*new_color))
```

Just set the color that was passed as an argument. That's it!

Defining the palette

Here comes the creative part: defining the actual palette. With all the groundwork in place, let's remove the old `RadioButton` definitions from `paint.kv` and start anew.

To use the familiar CSS notation for colors, we'll need to import the appropriate function into the `paint.kv` file. Yes, it can import functions, just like a regular Python module.

Add this line to the beginning of `paint.kv`:

```
#:import C kivy.utils.get_color_from_hex
```

This is exactly the same as the following code in Python (with shorter alias for brevity, since we're going to use it a lot):

```
from kivy.utils import get_color_from_hex as C
```

As mentioned earlier, we will use Flat UI colors for this example, but feel free to choose whatever palette you like. The definition itself looks like this:

```
BoxLayout:
    # ...
    ColorButton:
        background_color: C('#2980b9')
        state: 'down'
```

```
ColorButton:
    background_color: C('#16A085')

ColorButton:
    background_color: C('#27AE60')
```

This notation is as clear as it can possibly get. There is just one property to define for every `ColorButton` widget, namely its `background_color` property. Everything else is inherited from the class definition, including the event handler.

The beauty of this architecture is that now we can add any number of such buttons, and they will align and perform correctly.

Setting the line thickness

The last and easiest feature that we are going to implement is a simple line thickness selector. As you can see in the following screenshot, we're reusing assets and styles from the previous part, the color palette.

Line width selector

This UI uses yet another `RadioButton` subclass, unimaginatively named `LineWidthButton`. Append the following declaration to the `paint.kv` file:

```
<LineWidthButton@ColorButton>:
    group: 'line_width'
    on_release: app.canvas_widget.set_line_width(self.text)
    color: C('#2C3E50')
    background_color: C('#ECF0F1')
```

Key differences from `ColorButton` are highlighted in the preceding code. These new buttons belong to another radio group and fire another event handler when interacted with. Other than this, they are very similar.

The layout is equally simple, built in the same fashion as that of the color palette, except that it's vertical:

```
BoxLayout:
    orientation: 'vertical'
    padding: 2
    spacing: 2
    x: 0
    top: root.top
    width: 80
    height: 110

    LineWidthButton:
        text: 'Thin'

    LineWidthButton:
        text: 'Normal'
        state: 'down'

    LineWidthButton:
        text: 'Thick'
```

Note that our new event listener `CanvasWidget.set_line_width` will accept the `text` property of a pressed button. It is implemented like this for simplicity, as this allows us to define just one distinct property per widget.

In the real-world scenario, this approach isn't strictly forbidden or particularly unheard of but, still a bit questionable: what happens with these text labels when we decide to translate our application to Chinese or Hebrew?

Changing the line width

With every part of the user interface in place, we can finally attach the event listener that's going to apply the selected line thickness to the painting. We will store the numeric value of the line width in `CanvasWidget.line_width`, based on the button's text mapping that's provided inline, and use it in the `on_touch_down` handler when beginning a new line. Long story short, these are relevant parts of the revised `CanvasWidget` class:

```
class CanvasWidget(Widget):
    line_width = 2

    def on_touch_down(self, touch):
```

```
    # ...
    with self.canvas:
        touch.ud['current_line'] = Line(
            points=(touch.x, touch.y),
            width=self.line_width)

def set_line_width(self, line_width='Normal'):
    self.line_width = {
        'Thin': 1, 'Normal': 2, 'Thick': 4
    }[line_width]
```

This concludes the Kivy Paint app tutorial. If you start the program now, you can probably paint something beautiful. (I cannot, as you have probably noticed from the illustrations.)

Summary

In this chapter, we highlighted a number of common practices for the development of Kivy-based apps, such as customization of the main window, changing the mouse cursor, window size, and background color, the use of canvas instructions to draw free-form graphics programmatically, and handling touch events correctly across all supported platforms, with regards to multitouch.

One thing about Kivy that should be evident after building the Paint app is how open ended and versatile the framework is. Instead of providing a large number of rigid components, Kivy capitalizes on composability of simple building blocks: graphical primitives and behaviors. This means that while there are not many useful ready-made widgets bundled with Kivy, you can hack together anything you need in a few lines of highly readable Pythonic code.

The modular API design pays off nicely, thanks to its practically limitless flexibility. The end result meets your application's unique requirements perfectly. The customer wants something sensational, such as a triangular button—sure, you can also have a texture on it, all in a whopping three lines of code or so. (By comparison, try making a triangular button using **WinAPI**. That's like staring into the abyss, only less productive.)

These custom Kivy components also usually end up being reusable. In fact, you could easily import `CanvasWidget` from the `main.py` module and use it in another application.

Natural user interface

It's also worth mentioning that our second app is way more interactive than the first one: it responds not just to button clicks, but to arbitrary multitouch gestures as well.

All the available window surface reacts to touch, and as soon as it becomes evident to the end user, there is no cognitive overhead to painting, especially on a touch screen device. You just paint on a screen with your fingers, like it was a physical surface, and your fingers were sufficiently dirty to leave marks on it.

This kind of interface, or lack thereof, is called **NUI** (**natural user interface**). It has an interesting characteristic: a NUI application can be used by small kids and even pets—those capable of seeing and touching graphical objects on screen. This is literally a natural, intuitive interface, a "no-brainer" kind of thing, as opposed to the interface of, for example, Norton Commander, which was called intuitive back in the days. Let's face it: that was a lie. Intuition is not applicable to blue-screen, two-panel ASCII art programs in any practical way.

In the next chapter, we will build yet another Kivy-based program, this time limited to Android devices. It will exemplify the interoperability between Python code and Java classes that comprise the Android API.

Sound Recorder for Android

In the previous chapter, we briefly discussed how the Kivy app, generally cross-platform, may have parts of code working conditionally on selected systems, enhancing user experience for some users and performing other platform-specific tasks.

At times, this is essentially free; for example, multitouch just works if Kivy detects support for it on a target system—you don't need to write any code to turn it on, but only account for the sheer possibility of several pointer events firing at the same time for different touches.

Other platform-dependent tasks include code that just cannot run on other systems for various reasons. Remember the mouse cursor customization from the Paint app? That code used low-level bindings to SDL cursor routines provided by Pygame, which is perfectly fine as long as you have SDL and Pygame running. So, in order to make our app multi-platform, we took precautions to avoid entering that specific code path on incompatible systems; otherwise, it would have crashed our program.

Otherwise, Kivy applications are generally portable across all supported platforms—Mac, Windows, Linux, iOS, Android, and Raspberry Pi—with no significant problems. Until they aren't; we will discuss the reason for this in a second.

Kivy supports a wide variety of platforms

In this chapter, we're going to cover the following topics:

- Achieving interoperability between Python and Java using the **Pyjnius** library
- Testing Kivy apps on a device (or an emulator) running Android OS
- Working with Android's sound API from Python, which allows you to record and playback audio files
- Making a tiled user interface layout, similar in concept to Windows Phone
- Using icon fonts to improve the presentation of the app with vector icons

Writing platform-dependent code

Most of the projects in this book are inherently cross-platform, thanks to Kivy being extremely portable. This time, however, we're building an app that will be purposefully single-platform. This is certainly a severe limitation that reduces our potential user base; on the other hand, this gives us an opportunity to rely on platform-specific bindings that provide extended functionality.

The need for such bindings arises from the fact that Kivy strives to be as cross-platform as possible and delivers a similar user experience on every system it supports. This is a huge feature by itself; as a plus, we have the ability to write code once and run everywhere with little to no tweaks.

The downside of being cross-platform, however, is that you can only rely on the core functionality supported by every system. This "lowest common denominator" feature set includes rendering graphics on the screen, reproducing a sound if there is a sound card, accepting user input, and not much else.

Each Kivy app, by the virtue of being written in Python, also has access to the vast Python standard library. It facilitates networking, supports a number of application protocols, and provides many general-purpose algorithms and utility functions.

Still, the **input-output** (**IO**) capabilities of a "pure Kivy" program are limited to those that are present on most platforms. This amounts to a tiny fraction of what a common computer system, such as a smartphone or a tablet PC, can actually do.

Let's take a look at the API surface of a modern mobile device (for the sake of this chapter, let's assume it's running Android). We'll split everything in two parts: things that are supported directly by Python and/or Kivy, and things that aren't.

The following are features that are directly available in Python or Kivy:

- Hardware-accelerated graphics
- Touch screen input with optional multitouch

- Sound playback (at the time of writing this, the playback is supported only for files in persistent storage)
- Networking, assuming that Internet connectivity is present

The following are features that aren't supported or require an external library:

- Modem, support for voice calls, and SMS
- Use of built-in cameras for filming videos and taking pictures
- Use of a built-in microphone to record sound
- Cloud storage for application data, associated with a user account
- Bluetooth and other near-field networking features
- Location services and GPS
- Fingerprinting and other biometric security
- Motion sensors, that is, accelerometer and gyroscope
- Screen brightness control
- Vibration and other forms of haptic feedback
- Battery charge level

> For most entries in the "not supported" list, different Python libraries are already present to fill the gap, such as Audiostream for a low-level sound recording and Plyer that handles many platform-specific tasks.
>
> So, it's not like these features are completely unavailable to your application; realistically, the challenge is that these bits of functionality are insanely fragmented across different platforms (or even consecutive versions of the same platform, for example, Android); thus, you end up writing platform-specific, not portable code anyway.

As you can see from the preceding comparison, a lot of functionality is available on Android, only partially covered by an existing Python or Kivy API. This leaves a huge amount of untamed potential for using platform-specific features in your applications. This is not a limitation, but an opportunity. Shortly, you will learn how to utilize any Android API from Python code, allowing your Kivy application to do practically anything.

Another advantage of narrowing the scope of your app to only a small selection of systems is that there are whole new classes of programs that can function (or even make sense) only on a mobile device with fitting hardware specifications. These include augmented reality apps, gyroscope-controlled games, panoramic cameras, and so on.

Introducing Pyjnius

To harness the full power of our chosen platform, we're going to use a platform-specific API, which happens to be in Java and thus primarily Java-oriented. We are going to build a sound recorder app, similar to the apps commonly found in Android and iOS, albeit more simplistic. Unlike pure Kivy, the underlying Android API certainly provides us with ways of recording sound programmatically.

The rest of the chapter will cover this little recorder program throughout its development to illustrate the Python-Java interoperability using the excellent Pyjnius library, another great project made by Kivy developers. The concept we chose—sound recording and playback—is deliberately simple so as to outline the features of such interoperation without too much distraction caused by the sheer complexity of a subject and abundant implementation details.

The most interesting property of Pyjnius is that it doesn't provide its own "overlay" API over Android's, but instead allows you to use Java classes directly from Python. It means that you have full access to the native Android API and the official Android documentation, which is obviously more suited for Java development, not Python. However, this is still better than having no API reference at all.

Note that you don't have to install Pyjnius locally to complete the tutorial, since we obviously aren't going to run the code that taps into Android Java classes on the machine used for development.

The source code of Pyjnius, together with the reference manual and some examples, can be found in the official repository at `https://github.com/kivy/pyjnius`.

We will talk about Pyjnius only in the context of Android development and interoperation, but keep in mind that you can do the same kind of integration with desktop Java. This is an interesting property because another option of scripting a Java API from Python is Jython, which is rather slow and incomplete. Pyjnius, on the other hand, allows you to use the official Python interpreter (CPython), together with a multitude of libraries such as NumPy, which facilitates very fast computation.

So, if you absolutely have to call a Java library from Python, by all means consider Pyjnius as a good interop variant.

Emulating Android

As mentioned earlier, this chapter's project targets Android exclusively, thus it will not work on your computer. Don't worry if you haven't got a spare Android gadget, or if you don't feel comfortable toying with the real, physical device for the purpose of this tutorial. There are good-quality Android emulators available to help you overcome this minor obstacle and toy with the Android OS from the comfort of your desktop.

One of the best emulators out there is Genymotion (previously AndroVM), built on top of Oracle's VirtualBox virtual machine. You can grab a free copy from the official website, `http://www.genymotion.com/`; at the time of writing this, their licensing is very liberal, allowing for practically unrestricted free personal use.

The installation of the VM package is wildly different for every emulator and host OS combination, so we won't provide overly detailed instructions at this point. After all, these things are supposed to be user friendly nowadays, complete with instruction manuals and graphical user interfaces. Truly, we have reached the golden age of technology.

Even if the last sentence wasn't entirely sarcastic, there would've been some things to consider when setting up and using a virtual machine for Android emulation:

- Always use the latest version of Android. Backward compatibility or lack thereof can be pretty bad; debugging OS-level glitches isn't entertaining at all.

- Don't hesitate to search the Internet for solutions. The Android community is huge, and if you have a problem, it means that you're most probably not alone.

- The Kivy Launcher app, which you may find very useful to test your own programs, is available in the form of an `.apk` file from the official Kivy website, `http://kivy.org/`; this will be useful for emulated Android devices that don't have access to Google Play.

- Lastly, there are many different emulators out there of varying quality and compatibility. If things just seem to blow up and cease working at random, maybe you should try another VM or Android distribution. Fiddling with the virtual machine's configuration may also help.

The next screenshot depicts a Genymotion virtual machine running a recent version of Android, complete with usable Kivy Launcher:

Genymotion VM running Android 4.4.2 with Kivy
Launcher installed

Metro UI

While we're at it, let's build a user interface that resembles the Windows Phone home screen. This concept, basically a grid of colored rectangles (tiles) of various sizes, was known as **Metro UI** at some point in time, but was later renamed to **Modern UI** due to trademark issues. No matter the name, this is how it looks. This will give you a vague idea of what we'll be aiming at during the course of this app's development:

Design inspiration – Windows Phone home screen with tiles

Obviously, we aren't going to replicate it as is, but rather make something that resembles the depicted user interface. The following list pretty much summarizes the distinctive features we're after:

- Everything is aligned to a rectangular grid
- UI elements feature the same flat look discussed in *Chapter 1, Building a Clock App* (tiles use bright, solid colors, and there are no shadows or rounded corners)
- Tiles that are considered more useful (for an arbitrary definition of "useful") are larger and thus easier to hit

If this sounds easy to you, then you're absolutely right. As you will see shortly, the Kivy implementation of such a UI is rather straightforward.

The buttons

To start off, we are going to tweak a `Button` class, just like we did in our previous applications. It resembles `ColorButton` from the Paint app (*Chapter 2, Building a Paint App*):

```
<Button>:
    background_normal: 'button_normal.png'
    background_down: 'button_down.png'
    background_color: C('#95A5A6')
    font_size: 40
```

The texture we set as the background is solid white, exploiting the same trick that was used while creating the color palette. The `background_color` property acts as tint color, and assigning a plain white texture equals to painting the button in `background_color`. We don't want borders this time.

The second (pressed `background_down`) texture is 25 percent transparent white. Combined with the pitch-black background color of the app, we're getting a slightly darker shade of the same background color the button was assigned:

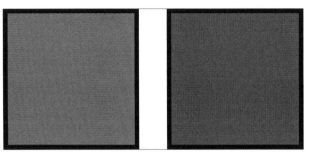

Normal (left) and pressed (right) states of a button – the background color is set to #0080FF

The grid structure

The layout is a bit more complex to build. In the absence of readily available Modern UI-like tiled layout, we are going to emulate it with the built-in `GridLayout` widget. It behaves just like the `BoxLayout` widget we used earlier, only in two dimensions instead of one, so there is no `orientation: 'horizontal'` or `'vertical'` property — the `GridLayout` widget is both at the same time.

One such layout could have fulfilled all our needs, if not for the last requirement: we want to have bigger and smaller buttons. Presently, `GridLayout` doesn't allow the merging of cells to create bigger ones (a functionality similar to the `rowspan` and `colspan` attributes in HTML would be nice to have). So, we will go in the opposite direction: start with the root `GridLayout` with big cells and add another `GridLayout` inside a cell to subdivide it.

Thanks to nested layouts working great in Kivy, we arrive at the following Kivy language structure (let's name the file `recorder.kv`):

```
#:import C kivy.utils.get_color_from_hex

GridLayout:
    padding: 15
```

```
Button:
    background_color: C('#3498DB')
    text: 'aaa'

GridLayout:
    Button:
        background_color: C('#2ECC71')
        text: 'bbb1'

    Button:
        background_color: C('#1ABC9C')
        text: 'bbb2'

    Button:
        background_color: C('#27AE60')
        text: 'bbb3'

    Button:
        background_color: C('#16A085')
        text: 'bbb4'

Button:
    background_color: C('#E74C3C')
    text: 'ccc'

Button:
    background_color: C('#95A5A6')
    text: 'ddd'
```

In order to run this code, you'll need the usual `main.py` boilerplate to serve as an application's entry point. Try writing this code yourself as an exercise.

 Refer to the beginning of the first chapter. The application class name will be different because it should reflect the name of the Kivy language file presented earlier.

Note how the nested `GridLayout` widget sits on the same level as that of outer, large buttons. This should make perfect sense if you look at the previous screenshot of the WinPhone home screen: a pack of four smaller buttons takes up the same space (one outer grid cell) as a large button. The nested `GridLayout` is a container for those smaller buttons.

Visual attributes

On the outer grid, `padding` is provided to create some distance from the edges of the screen. Other visual attributes are shared between `GridLayout` instances and moved to a class, resulting in the following code inside `recorder.kv`:

```
<GridLayout>:
    cols: 2
    spacing: 10
    row_default_height:
        (0.5 * (self.width - self.spacing[0]) -
        self.padding[0])
    row_force_default: True
```

 It's worth mentioning that both `padding` and `spacing` are effectively lists, not scalars. The `spacing[0]` property refers to a horizontal spacing, followed by a vertical one. However, we can initialize `spacing` with a single value, as shown in the preceding code; this value will then be used for everything.

Each grid consists of two columns with some spacing in between. The `row_default_height` property is trickier: we can't just say, "Let the row height be equal to the cell width." Instead, we compute the desired height manually, where 0.5 is because we have two columns:

$$row\ height = 0.5 \times (screen\ width - all\ padding\ and\ spacing)$$

If we don't apply this tweak, the buttons inside the grid will fill all the available vertical space, which is undesirable, especially when there aren't that many buttons (every one of them ends up being too large). Instead, we want all the buttons nice and square, with empty space at the bottom left, well, empty.

The following is the screenshot of our app's "Modern UI" tiles, resulting from the preceding code:

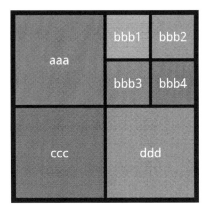

The UI so far – clickable tiles of variable size
not too dissimilar from our design inspiration

Scalable vector icons

One of the nice finishing touches we can apply to the application UI is the use of icons, and not just text, on buttons. We could, of course, just throw in a bunch of images, but let's borrow another useful technique from modern web development and use an icon font instead – as you will see shortly, these provide great flexibility at no cost.

Icon fonts

Icon fonts are essentially just like regular ones, except their glyphs are unrelated to the letters of a language. For example, you type "P" and the Python logo is rendered instead of the letter; every font invents its own mnemonic on how to assign letters to icons.

This is about the only downside to using an icon font – the code that uses such font heavily isn't very readable because character–icon mapping is hardly obvious. This can be mitigated by using constants instead of entering symbols directly.

There are also fonts that don't use English letters, instead they map icons to Unicode's "private use area" character codes. This is a technically correct way to build such a font, but application support for this Unicode feature varies – not every platform behaves the same in this regard, especially when it comes to mobile platforms. The font that we will use for our app does not assign private use characters and uses ASCII (plain English letters) instead.

Rationale for using icon fonts

On the Web, icon fonts solve a number of problems that are commonly associated with (raster) images:

- First and foremost, raster images don't scale well and may become blurry when resized — there are certain algorithms that produce better results than others, but as of today, the "state of the art" is still not perfect. In contrast, a vector picture is infinitely scalable, by definition.

- Raster image files containing schematic graphics (such as icons and UI elements) tend to be larger than vector formats. This does not apply to photos encoded as JPEG, obviously.

- In addition, an icon font is typically just one file for any number of icons, which means one HTTP round trip. Regular icons (images) routinely end up in separate files, leading to significant HTTP overhead; there are ways to mitigate this, such as CSS sprites, but they are not universally used and have their own problems.

- In the case of icon fonts, a color change literally takes about a second — you can do just that by adding `color: red` (for example) to your CSS file. The same is true for size, rotation, and other properties that don't involve changing the geometry of an image. Effectively, this means that making trivial adjustments to an icon does not require an image editor, like it normally would when dealing with bitmaps.

Some of these points do not apply to Kivy apps that much, but overall, the use of icon fonts is considered a good practice in contemporary web development, especially since there are many free high-quality fonts to choose from — that's hundreds of icons readily available for inclusion in your project.

Two great sources of free fonts (including those that are free for commercial usage) are **Font Squirrel** (`http://www.fontsquirrel.com`) and **Google Fonts** (`https://www.google.com/fonts`). Never mind the general web development orientation of these sites, most fonts are just as usable in your offline programs as they are on the Web. If not more so, because browser support still isn't ideal.

The only thing that really matters is the file format: Kivy only supports True Type (`.ttf`) at the moment. Thankfully, this is the most popular font format out there anyway. Besides, it's possible to convert a font from practically any other format to `.ttf`.

Using the icon font in Kivy

In our application, we are going to use the Modern Pictograms (version 1) free font, designed by John Caserta. The following is a glimpse of how it looks:

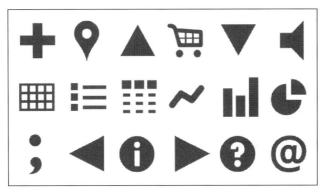

A small sample of icons from the Modern Pictograms icon font

To load the font into our Kivy program, we'll use the same process outlined in *Chapter 1*, *Building a Clock App*. In this specific case, it isn't strictly necessary, as icon fonts rarely have different font weights and styles. Still, accessing the font by display name (Modern Pictograms) rather than the filename (modernpics.ttf) is a better way. You can later rename or move the font file by updating just one occurrence of its path, and not every place where the font was used.

The code so far (in main.py) looks like this:

```
from kivy.app import App
from kivy.core.text import LabelBase

class RecorderApp(App):
    pass

if __name__ == '__main__':
    LabelBase.register(name='Modern Pictograms',
                       fn_regular='modernpics.ttf')

    RecorderApp().run()
```

The actual use of the font happens inside `recorder.kv`. First, we want to update the `Button` class once again to allow us to change the font in the middle of a text using markup tags. This is shown in the following code snippet:

```
<Button>:
    background_normal: 'button_normal.png'
    background_down: 'button_down.png'
    font_size: 24
    halign: 'center'
    markup: True
```

The `halign: 'center'` attribute means that we want every line of text centered inside the button. The `markup: True` attribute is self-evident and required because the next step in customization of buttons will rely heavily on markup.

Now we can update button definitions. Here's an example of this:

```
Button:
    background_color: C('#3498DB')
    text:
        ('[font=Modern Pictograms][size=120]'
        'e[/size][/font]\nNew recording')
```

Normally, you don't need parentheses around strings in Kivy language files; this syntax is useful only when the declaration is multiline. This notation is effectively the same as writing a long string on the same line.

Notice the character `'e'` inside the `[font][size]` tags. That's the icon code. Every button in our app will use a different icon, and changing an icon amounts to replacing a single letter in the `recorder.kv` file. Complete mapping of the code for the Modern Pictograms font can be found on its official website at `http://modernpictograms.com/`.

In order to explore an icon font by hand, you'll need to use a font viewer. Typically, there is one readily available on your machine, regardless of an operating system.

- The **Character Map** program is bundled with Windows
- On a Mac, there is a built-in application called **Font Book**
- Linux has several viewers depending on the desktop environment of your choice, for example, **gnome-font-viewer** in GNOME

Alternatively, just search the Web. Popular fonts usually have some sort of user manual online that explains character mapping.

Long story short, this is how the UI of our application looks after the addition of icons to buttons:

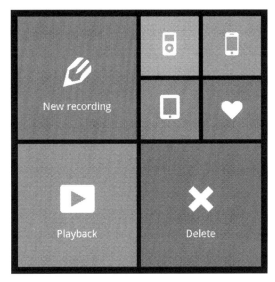

The sound recorder app interface – a modern UI with
vector icons from the Modern Pictograms font

This is already pretty close to the original Modern UI look.

You might wonder what is the purpose of smaller green buttons at the top-right corner. The answer is that currently they're there for quantity alone. Three buttons that we actually need to implement a sound recorder—record, play, delete—just aren't enough to illustrate the Modern UI concept, as it needs more diversity to look even remotely interesting.

Testing on Android

Right now, our app still doesn't contain any non-portable code, but let's gradually move towards our platform of choice nevertheless and begin testing it on Android. The only prerequisite for this operation is an Android device, physical or virtualized, with the **Kivy Launcher** application installed and working.

Packaging an app for Kivy Launcher is borderline trivial. We're going to add two files, `android.txt` and `icon.png`, to the same folder where other sources (in this case, `main.py` and `recorder.kv`) reside and then copy the folder to an SD card of the Android device under `/Kivy`. The directory structure should look something like the following:

SD card directory structure for Kivy Launcher

When you start Kivy Launcher, it will spell out the full path that it searches for projects. This may be useful, for example, when you have no SD card.

The format of the `android.txt` file is pretty self-evident:

```
title=App Name
author=Your Name
orientation=portrait
```

Title and author fields are just strings displayed in the list of apps. Orientation can be either portrait (vertical, *height > width*) or landscape (horizontal, *width > height*), depending on the application's preferred aspect ratio.

The icon `icon.png` is optional and will be blank if omitted. It is advisable to add it because it's much easier to look up applications based on their icons, and if you're planning to release the resulting app to the Google Play store, you'll need an icon anyway.

Note that the icon's filename isn't customizable, and neither is the `main.py` filename, which must designate the application's entry point; otherwise, Kivy Launcher won't start the app.

With all the files in place, you should see your Sound recorder program in the list when you start Kivy Launcher:

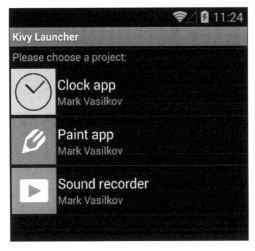

The Kivy Launcher applications list, containing every
app we've written during the course of this book

 If instead you see a message containing instructions where to put files, please recheck your paths — unfortunately, the directory that Kivy Launcher searches for projects is not easily configurable at the time of writing this. This may improve in future versions.

Now you can start your app by tapping the corresponding entry in the list. This is the easiest way to test a Kivy program on Android—just copy files and you're all set (as opposed to packaging an .apk file, which is also relatively straightforward but considerably more involved).

Using the native API

Having done the user interface part of the app, we will now turn to a native API and implement the sound recording and playback logic using the suitable Android Java classes, MediaRecorder and MediaPlayer.

Technically, both Python and Java are object-oriented, and it may even appear at first glance that these languages are rather similar. The utilization of OOP principles, however, differs radically. In comparison to Python, many Java APIs suffer from (or enjoy immensely, depending on who you ask) over-architecting and general overuse of the object-oriented paradigm. So don't be surprised that otherwise very simple tasks may require you to import and instantiate quite a lot of classes.

In 1913, Vladimir Lenin wrote regarding the Java architecture:

And there is only one way of smashing the resistance of those classes, and that is to find, in the very society which surrounds us, the forces which can constitute the power capable of sweeping away the old and creating the new.

The essay didn't mention Python or Pyjnius back then, but the message is clear—even a century ago, going overboard with classes wasn't very much welcome in the contemporary society.

Thankfully, the task at hand is relatively simple. To record a sound using the Android API, we only need the following five Java classes:

- `android.os.Environment`: This class provides access to many useful environment variables. We are going to use it to determine the path where SD card is mounted so we can save the recorded audio file. It's tempting to just hardcode `'/sdcard/'` or a similar constant, but in practice, every other Android device has a different filesystem layout. So let's not do this even for the purposes of the tutorial.

- `android.media.MediaRecorder`: This class is our main workhorse. It facilitates capturing audio and video and saving it to the filesystem.

- `android.media.MediaRecorder$AudioSource`, `android.media.MediaRecorder$AudioEncoder`, and `android.media.MediaRecorder$OutputFormat`: These are enumerations that hold values we need to pass as arguments to the various methods of `MediaRecorder`.

Java class naming scheme

The dollar sign in the class name commonly means that the class is internal. This is not the exact heuristic, as you can declare a similar class name yourself without following any logic whatsoever—`'$'` is a usable character in Java variable and class names, not too dissimilar from, for example, JavaScript. Such unorthodox naming, however, is frowned upon.

Loading Java classes

The code to load the aforementioned Java classes into your Python application is as follows:

```
from jnius import autoclass

Environment = autoclass('android.os.Environment')
MediaRecorder = autoclass('android.media.MediaRecorder')
AudioSource = autoclass('android.media.MediaRecorder$AudioSource')
OutputFormat = autoclass('android.media.MediaRecorder$OutputFormat')
AudioEncoder = autoclass('android.media.MediaRecorder$AudioEncoder')
```

If you try to run the program at this point, you'll receive an error, something along the lines of:

- **ImportError: No module named jnius**: You'll encounter this error if you don't have Pyjnius installed on your machine

- **jnius.JavaException: Class not found 'android/os/Environment'**: You'll encounter this error if Pyjnius is installed, but the Android classes we're trying to load are missing (for example, when running on a desktop machine)

This is one of the rare cases when receiving an error means we did everything right. From now on, we should do all of the testing on Android device or inside an emulator because the code isn't cross-platform anymore. It relies unequivocally on Android-specific Java features.

Now we can use Java classes seamlessly in our Python code.

> Keep in mind that the documentation for these classes is intended for use with Java, not Python. You can look it up on Google's official Android developers portal at http://developer.android.com/reference/packages.html — translating code samples from Java to Python may appear intimidating at first, but in reality, it is dead simple (if a bit wordy).

Looking up the storage path

Let's illustrate the practical cross-language API use with a simple example. In Java, we would do something like this in order to find out where an SD card is mounted:

```
import android.os.Environment;

String path = Environment.getExternalStorageDirectory()
.getAbsolutePath();
```

When translated to Python, this code reads:

```
Environment = autoclass('android.os.Environment')
path = Environment.getExternalStorageDirectory().getAbsolutePath()
```

This is the exact same thing as shown in the previous code, only written in Python instead of Java.

While we're at it, let's also log this value, so that we can see in the Kivy log which exact path the `getAbsolutePath` method returned to our code:

```
from kivy.logger import Logger
Logger.info('App: storage path == "%s"' % path)
```

On my testing device, this produces the following line in the Kivy log:

```
[INFO] App: storage path == "/storage/sdcard0"
```

Reading logs from the device

When you're running a Kivy application from the terminal during development, logs appear immediately in the same terminal window. This very useful feature is also available, albeit less accessible, when your app runs inside Kivy Launcher.

To read Kivy logs, navigate to the folder where your app lives on the device (for example, `/Kivy/Recorder` on the SD card). Inside this folder, Kivy Launcher creates another directory named `.kivy`, with the default configuration and miscellaneous service information inside. Every time the application is started, a log file is created under `.kivy/logs`.

Alternatively, if you have the Android SDK installed, you can enable USB debugging on your device and then use the `adb logcat` command to see all the Android logs, including Kivy logs, in one place. This produces much more information about the internal processes happening inside the device, such as various hardware activating and deactivating, application windows changing their state, and so on.

Logs can be of tremendous value when debugging strange program behavior or when an app just refuses to start. Kivy also prints all sorts of warnings about the runtime environment there, such as libraries or features missing, Python modules failing to load, and other potential problems.

Recording sound

Now, let's dive deeper into the rabbit hole of the Android API and actually record a sound from the mic. The following code is again basically a translation of Android API documentation into Python. If you're interested in the original Java version of this code, you may find it at `http://developer.android.com/guide/topics/media/audio-capture.html` — it's way too lengthy to include here.

The following is the preparation code that initializes a `MediaRecorder` object:

```
storage_path = (Environment.getExternalStorageDirectory()
                   .getAbsolutePath() + '/kivy_recording.3gp')

recorder = MediaRecorder()

def init_recorder():
    recorder.setAudioSource(AudioSource.MIC)
    recorder.setOutputFormat(OutputFormat.THREE_GPP)
    recorder.setAudioEncoder(AudioEncoder.AMR_NB)
    recorder.setOutputFile(storage_path)
    recorder.prepare()
```

This is the typical, straightforward, verbose Java way of initializing things, rewritten in Python word for word.

You can tweak the output file format and codec here, for example, change `AMR_NB` (**Adaptive Multi-Rate** codec, which is optimized for speech and hence widely used in GSM and other mobile phone networks) to `AudioEncoder.AAC` (**Advanced Audio Coding** standard, a more general-purpose codec similar to MP3). There is probably no good reason for this since the dynamic range of the built-in microphone is unlikely to be suitable for recording music anyway, but the choice is yours.

Now for the fun part, the "Begin/End recording" button. The following code snippet uses the same logic as already seen in *Chapter 1, Building a Clock App*, when implementing the Start/Stop button for the stopwatch:

```
class RecorderApp(App):
    is_recording = False

    def begin_end_recording(self):
        if (self.is_recording):
            recorder.stop()
            recorder.reset()
            self.is_recording = False
            self.root.ids.begin_end_recording.text = \
                ('[font=Modern Pictograms][size=120]'
```

```
                    'e[/size][/font]\nBegin recording')
        return

    init_recorder()
    recorder.start()
    self.is_recording = True
    self.root.ids.begin_end_recording.text = \
        ('[font=Modern Pictograms][size=120]'
         '%[/size][/font]\nEnd recording')
```

As you can see, no rocket science was applied here either: we just stored the current state, `is_recording`, and then took the action depending on it, namely:

1. Start or stop the `MediaRecorder` object (the highlighted part).

2. Flip the `is_recording` flag.

3. Update the button text so that it reflects the current state (see the following screenshot).

The last part of the application that needs updating is the `recorder.kv` file. We need to tweak the "Begin/End recording" button so that it calls our `begin_end_recording()` function:

```
Button:
        id: begin_end_recording
        background_color: C('#3498DB')
        text:
            ('[font=Modern Pictograms][size=120]'
             'e[/size][/font]\nBegin recording')
        on_press: app.begin_end_recording()
```

That's it! If you run the application now, chances are that you'll be able to actually record a sound file that is going to be stored on the SD card. However, please see the next section before you do this. The button that you created will look something like the following:

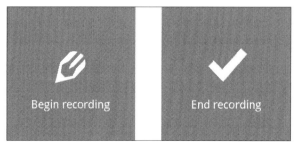

Begin recording and End recording – this one button
summarizes our app's functionality so far

Major caveat – permissions

The default Kivy Launcher app at the time of writing this doesn't have the necessary permission to record sound, `android.permission.RECORD_AUDIO`. This results in a crash as soon as the `MediaRecorder` instance is initialized.

There are many ways to mitigate this problem. First, the easiest one: for the sake of this tutorial, we already provide a modified Kivy Launcher that has the necessary permission enabled. You can find `KivyLauncherMod.apk` bundled with the book's source code archive. The latest version of the package is also available for download at `https://github.com/mvasilkov/kivy_launcher_hack`.

Before you install the provided `.apk` file, please delete the existing version of the app, if any, from your device.

Alternatively, if you're willing to fiddle with the gory details of bundling Kivy apps for Google Play, you can build Kivy Launcher yourself from the source code. Everything you need to do this can be found in the official Kivy GitHub account, `https://github.com/kivy`.

The third viable option (also probably easier than the previous one) is to tweak the already existing Kivy Launcher app. To do so, you can use the **apktool** (`https://code.google.com/p/android-apktool/`). The exact steps you need to take are outlined as follows:

1. Download the official `KivyLauncher.apk` file and extract it from the command line, assuming that the apktool is in your path:

   ```
   apktool d -b -s -d KivyLauncher.apk KivyLauncher
   ```

2. Add the necessary permission statement to the `AndroidManifest.xml` file:

   ```
   <uses-permission android:name="android.permission.RECORD_AUDIO" />
   ```

3. Repackage `.apk` like this:

   ```
   apktool b KivyLauncher KivyLauncherWithChanges.apk
   ```

4. Sign the resulting `.apk` file using the `jarsigner` utility. Have a look at the official documentation on signing Android packages, available at `http://developer.android.com/tools/publishing/app-signing.html#signing-manually`.

As a result of this procedure, the modified Kivy Launcher package will be able to record sound.

You can add various other permissions in the same way to be able to exploit them in your Python code using Pyjnius. For example, in order to access the GPS API, your app needs the `android.permission.ACCESS_FINE_LOCATION` permission.

All available permissions are listed in the Android documentation at `http://developer.android.com/reference/android/Manifest.permission.html`.

Playing sound

Getting sound playback to work is easier; there is no permission for this, and the API is somewhat more concise too. We need to load just one more class, `MediaPlayer`:

```
MediaPlayer = autoclass('android.media.MediaPlayer')
player = MediaPlayer()
```

The following is the code that will run when the user presses the Play button. We'll also use the `reset_player()` function in the *Deleting files* section; otherwise, there could have been one slightly longer function:

```
def reset_player():
    if (player.isPlaying()):
        player.stop()
    player.reset()

def restart_player():
    reset_player()
    try:
        player.setDataSource(storage_path)
        player.prepare()
        player.start()
    except:
        player.reset()
```

The intricate details of each API call can be found in the official documentation, but overall, this listing is pretty self-evident: reset the player to its initial state, load the sound file, and push play. The file format is determined automatically, making our task at hand a wee bit easier.

In practice, such code should always be wrapped in a `try ...` `catch` block. There are just too many things that can go wrong: the file may go missing or created in a wrong format, the SD card may become unplugged or otherwise unreadable, and other equally terrible things that will surely crash your program if given a chance. A good rule of thumb when doing IO is *better safe than sorry*.

Deleting files

This last feature will use the `java.io.File` class, which is not strictly related to Android. One great thing about the official Android documentation is that it contains reference to these core Java classes too, despite the fact they predate the Android operating system by more than a decade. The actual code needed to implement file removal is exactly one line; it's highlighted in the following listing:

```
File = autoclass('java.io.File')

class RecorderApp(App):
    def delete_file(self):
        reset_player()
        File(storage_path).delete()
```

First, we stop the playback (if any) by calling the `reset_player()` function, and then remove the file — short and sweet.

Interestingly, the `File.delete()` method in Java won't throw an exception in the event of a catastrophic failure, so there is no need to perform `try ... catch` in this case. Consistency, consistency everywhere.

> An attentive reader will notice that we could also delete the file using Python's own `os.remove()` function. Doing this using Java achieves nothing special compared to a pure Python implementation; it's also slower. On the other hand, as a demonstration of Pyjnius, `java.io.File` works as good as any other Java class.
>
> Also note that this function will run perfectly fine in a desktop OS as well because it's not Android-specific; you only need Java and Pyjnius installed in order for this to work.

At this point, with the UI and all three major functions done, our application is complete for the purposes of this tutorial.

Summary

Writing non-portable code has its strengths and weaknesses, just like any other global architectural decision. This particular choice, however, is especially hard because the switch to native API typically happens early in the project and may be completely impractical to undo at a later stage.

The major advantage of the approach was discussed at the beginning of this chapter: with platform-specific code, you can do virtually anything that your platform is capable of. There are no artificial limits; your Python code has unrestricted access to the same underlying API as the native code.

On the downside, depending on a single platform is risky for a number of reasons:

- The market of Android alone is provably smaller than that of Android plus iOS (this holds true for about every combination of operating systems).

- Porting the program over to a new system becomes harder with every platform-specific feature you use.

- If the project runs on just one platform, exactly one political decision may be sufficient to kill it. The chances of getting banned by Google is higher than that of getting the boot from both App Store and Google Play simultaneously. (Again, this holds true for practically every set of application marketplaces.)

Now that you're well aware of the options, it's up to you to make an educated choice regarding every app you develop.

A few words on the UI

By all means, you should not hesitate to borrow and re-implement ideas (and layouts, fonts, colors, and so on) seen elsewhere. The phrase attributed to Pablo Picasso, "Good artists borrow; great artists steal," summarizes today's web and application development neatly. (The "steal" part is figurative: please don't actually steal things.)

Also, let's get this straight: the mere fact that Microsoft decided to use the "Modern UI" in a number of latest products, both mobile and desktop, doesn't mean that the design itself is any good. What we know for sure is that this user interface paradigm will be immediately recognizable by users due to popularity, fortunate or otherwise, of Microsoft operating systems.

Putting Java to rest, in the next chapter we will build a simple chat with client–server architecture on top of the popular Python web framework, **Twisted**.

4
Kivy Networking

Previously, we talked about trade-offs such as narrowing the application compatibility while aiming to broaden its feature set, for example, an Android-only application using the native API to do the heavy lifting. Now, let's explore the opposite extreme and build an app based on uncompromising, universally available functionality—networking.

In this chapter, we are going to build a Chat app, which is similar in concept to an **Internet Relay Chat (IRC)**, but much simpler.

While certainly not a replacement for enterprise-scale behemoths like Skype, by the end of this chapter, our little app will support multi-user messaging over the Internet. This is sufficient for small and friendly groups of people.

Being friendly is actually a requirement, as we're intentionally simplifying things by not implementing authentication. This means that users are able to easily impersonate each other. Tweaking the application to sustain hostile environments and catastrophic events (such as a political debate) is left for you to do, if you feel particularly adventurous.

We're also aiming at the widest possible compatibility, at least on the server side; you will be able to use even **Telnet** to send and receive messages. While not as pretty as graphical Kivy apps, Telnet runs perfectly fine in Windows 95 and even MS-DOS. Chat with dinosaurs!

 To be more historically accurate, the Telnet protocol was standardized in 1973, so it even predates the 8086 CPU and the x86 architecture. MS-DOS is much more modern in comparison, and Windows 95 is practically the future of computing.

The following important topics will be covered in this chapter:

- Writing and testing a custom server in Python, using the **Twisted** framework
- Developing a couple of client apps on different levels of abstraction, from simple terminal program using raw sockets to an event-driven Twisted client
- Using Kivy `ScreenManager` to better organize the application UI
- Employing a `ScrollView` container to efficiently present lengthy widgets on the screen

Our application will feature the centralized, client-server architecture; such topology is very common on the Internet, and many websites and applications work this way. As you will see shortly, it's also rather easy to implement as opposed to a decentralized, peer-to-peer network.

For the purposes of this chapter we don't differentiate a **local area network** (**LAN**) from the Internet, as it's largely irrelevant at this level of abstraction. However, note that deploying your application for large-scale consumption on the Internet, if done properly, requires knowledge in many additional areas, from setting up a secure web server and configuring the firewall to making the code scale across many processor cores and even several physical machines. In practice this may be less scary than it sounds, but still constitutes a nontrivial endeavor per se.

Writing the chat server

Let's start the development with the server-side code so that we have an endpoint to connect to before we begin writing the client. For this, we'll use an excellent **Twisted** framework that reduces many common, low-level networking tasks to a small number of lines of clean, relatively high-level Python code.

Compatibility notice

Twisted doesn't support Python 3 at the time of writing, so we'll assume that all the following Python code is intended to run on Python 2.7. It should be easy to port it to Python 3 eventually, as no deliberately incompatible design decisions are made. (On a related note, we'll also completely ignore Unicode-related issues, because resolving them properly depends on Python version.)

Twisted is an event-driven, low-level server framework, not unlike **Node.js** (in fact, Node.js design was influenced by Twisted). Quite similar to Kivy, the event-driven architecture means that we don't structure the code as a loop; instead, we bind a number of event listeners to the events that we deem useful for our app. Hardcore, low-level networking, such as handling incoming connections and working with raw data packets, is performed by Twisted automatically as soon as we start the server.

In order to install Twisted on your machine, run the usual command in the terminal:

```
pip install -U twisted
```

There are a few caveats:

- Chances are, you'll need to become root (administrator or "super user") to perform a system-wide installation. If you're on Mac OS or Linux, try prefixing the command with `sudo` if you receive an **Access Denied** error message.
- In the event you don't have pip installed, try the **easy_install twisted** command (or **easy_install pip**, for that matter).
- Alternatively, please follow the official pip installation guide at `https://pip.pypa.io/en/latest/installing.html`. This covers Windows too.

The protocol definition

Let's talk about the protocol that we are going to use to communicate with the chat server. Since the application is going to be very unsophisticated, instead of using a full-fledged extensive protocol such as XMPP, we're going to create our own barebones protocol containing only the bits we need.

In the context of this tutorial, there are just two messages passed from client to server that we want to implement on the protocol level—connecting to server (entering the chatroom), and actually talking to other users. Everything that the server sends back to the client is rendered; no service events originate on the server.

Our protocol will be textual, like many other application-level protocols, including the universally used HTTP. This is a very practical property because it makes debugging and related activities easier. Text protocols are also generally considered more extensible and future-proof, as opposed to binary ones. The downside of plain text is mainly its size; binary enumeration tends to be more compact. This is largely irrelevant in this case and can be easily mitigated anyway using compression (this is exactly what many servers do in case of HTTP).

Now let's review the individual messages that comprise our application's protocol:

- Connecting to the server communicates no other information except the fact that the user is now in the chat room, so we'll send just the word CONNECT every time. This message is not parameterized.

- Talking in the chat room is more interesting. There are two parameters: the nickname and the text message itself. Let's define the format of such message as A:B, where A is the nickname (as a direct consequence, the nickname can't contain the colon : character).

From this specification, we can derive an effective algorithm (pseudo code):

```
if ':' not in message
    then
        // it's a CONNECT message
        add this connection to user list
    else
        // it's a chat message
        nickname, text := message.split on ':'
        for each user in user list
            if not the same user:
                send "{nickname} said: {text}"
```

Testing for the same user is meant to cut the unnecessary transmission of users' own messages back to them (echo).

The server source code

With the help of the Twisted framework, our pseudocode can be translated into Python pretty much literally. The following listing contains the full source code of our server.py application:

```
from twisted.internet import protocol, reactor

transports = set()
```

```python
class Chat(protocol.Protocol):
    def dataReceived(self, data):
        transports.add(self.transport)

        if ':' not in data:
            return

        user, msg = data.split(':', 1)

        for t in transports:
            if t is not self.transport:
                t.write('{0} says: {1}'.format(user, msg))

class ChatFactory(protocol.Factory):
    def buildProtocol(self, addr):
        return Chat()

reactor.listenTCP(9096, ChatFactory())
reactor.run()
```

The principle of operation

This is the control flow outline that will help you understand exactly how our server works:

- The last line, `reactor.run()`, starts the `ChatFactory` server that listens on port 9096
- When the server receives input, it invokes the `dataReceived()` callback
- The `dataReceived()` method implements the pseudocode from the protocol section, sending messages to other connected clients as required

The set of connections to clients is called `transports`. We're adding the current transport, `self.transport`, to the set unconditionally, because in the case of existing element that's a no-op, so why bother.

The rest of the listing follows the algorithm exactly. As a result, every connected user except for the one who sent the original message will receive a notification, **<username>** says: **<message text>**.

Notice how we didn't actually check that the connect message says CONNECT. That's an example of closely following the *network robustness* principle, coined by Jon Postel in the TCP specification in 1980: *be conservative in what you send, and liberal in what you accept.*

In addition to simplifying the code in this case, we're also gaining an option for a forward compatibility. Let's say that in the future release of the client, we've added a new message to the protocol, namely the imaginary WHARRGARBL message that does, according to its name, something truly amazing. Instead of crashing due to receiving a malformed message (in this case, because of version mismatch), an old revision of the server will just ignore such messages and continue functioning.

Specifically this aspect — compatibility between versions — can be easily handled using a number of strategies. However, there are also more difficult problems when it comes to networking and especially public networks, including malicious users trying to defeat your system and bring it down on purpose. So, practically, there is no such thing as exaggerated server stability.

Testing the server

Run the server as you usually run any Python program:

```
python server.py
```

This command shouldn't produce any visible output. The server just sits there, waiting quietly for clients to connect. However, there are no client programs in the known universe that can speak this protocol, since we've made it all up about page and a half ago. How can we make sure that the server works?

Thankfully, this chicken and egg problem is so common in this field that there are many useful tools to do just that — send arbitrary bytes to any server, and receive and display arbitrary bytes that server sends back.

One of the standard programs suitable for fiddling with servers that use text protocols is Telnet. Like many "old school" Unix-style utilities, Telnet is a command-line program that can be used both interactively and as part of larger batch (shell) script.

Most operating systems come with the `telnet` command preinstalled. If it isn't, chances are that you're on MS Windows version 7 or greater. In this case, you can go to **Control Panel | Programs and Features | Turn Windows features on or off**, as shown in the following screenshot:

Then, make sure that the **Telnet Client** checkbox is on, as follows:

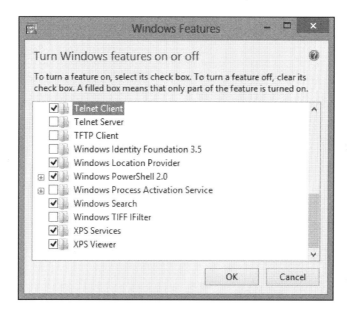

Telnet accepts two arguments: host name and port number of the server to connect to. In order to connect to the chat server with telnet, you'll need to start `server.py` first, and then in another terminal run:

```
telnet 127.0.0.1 9096
```

Alternatively, you can use `localhost` for host name on most systems, as this is synonymous with `127.0.0.1`; both denote the current machine.

If all went well, you will have an interactive session open where every line you type is sent to the server. Now, using the chat protocol that we discussed earlier, you can communicate with the server:

```
CONNECT
User A:Hello, world!
```

There will be no output, because we programmed the server in such a way that it doesn't echo messages back to their original author—that will be wasteful. So, let's open yet another terminal (and a Telnet session) so that we have two simultaneously connected users.

This is what the chat session looks like when everything is functioning properly:

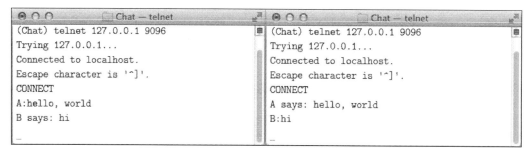

An interactive chat over the network at its finest

If for some reason, technical or otherwise, you cannot use Telnet on your system, please don't feel particularly bad about this, as this test is not required to successfully complete the tutorial.

However, here's some (very personal, intimate even) advice that is more related to your career than to the topic of this book: do yourself a favor and get a Mac OS or Linux box, or maybe use dual-boot on the same machine. These Unix-like operating systems are much better suited for software development than Windows, and the productivity boost is totally worth the inconvenience of getting used to a new environment.

With this we can conclude that our server works: two Telnet windows are talking just fine. Now that we're done with the backend, let's build a cross-platform GUI chat client.

Screen manager

Let's begin the UI development with a new concept, namely screen management. Our application at hand, the chat client, is a fitting example. There will be two application states with different UI that are completely separate from one another:

- The login screen where the user enters the hostname to connect to and the desired nickname:

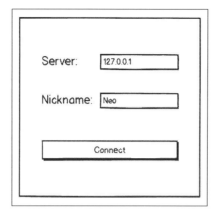

- The chatroom screen, where the actual conversation takes place:

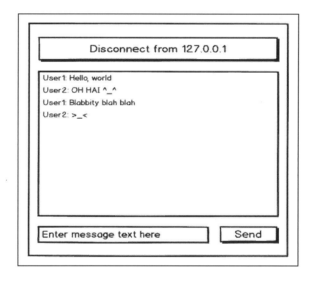

Conceptually, these are the application states of the Chat app's frontend.

A straightforward approach to such UI separation will amount to managing the visible and hidden controls depending on some variable that holds the current desired UI state. This gets cumbersome very quickly as the number of widgets grow, and the boilerplate code isn't exactly fun to write anyway.

That's why the Kivy framework provides us with a container widget specifically tailored for the task, ScreenManager. Additionally, ScreenManager supports short animations to visualize the screen change, with a number of prebuilt transitions to choose from. It can be used from a Kivy language file in a completely declarative manner without touching the Python code.

Let's do just that. Add the following code in the `chat.kv` file:

```
ScreenManager:
    Screen:
        name: 'login'

        BoxLayout:
            # other UI controls -- not shown

            Button:
                text: 'Connect'
                on_press: root.current = 'chatroom'

    Screen:
        name: 'chatroom'

        BoxLayout:
            # other UI controls -- not shown

            Button:
                text: 'Disconnect'
                on_press: root.current = 'login'
```

This is the basic structure of the program: we have a `ScreenManager` at the root and a `Screen` container for every UI state we want to have (the first one will be displayed by default). Inside the `Screen` is the usual UI: layouts, buttons, and everything we've seen so far. We'll get to it in a bit.

The code we just saw also includes screen-changing buttons, one per `Screen` instance. In order to switch the application state, we need to assign the desired screen's name to the `current` property of `ScreenManager`.

Customizing the animation

As stated previously, the brief animation that happens when changing screens can be customized. Kivy provides a number of such animations out of the box, found inside the `kivy.uix.screenmanager` package:

Transition class name	Visual effect
NoTransition	No animation, just displays the new screen immediately.
SlideTransition	Slides the new screen. Pass `'left'` (the default), `'right'`, `'up'`, or `'down'` to select the direction of the effect.
SwapTransition	In theory, this class simulates the iOS screen-swapping animation. The actual effect looks nothing like that though.

Transition class name	Visual effect
FadeTransition	Fades the screen out, then fades it back in.
WipeTransition	A smooth directional transition using a pixel shader.
FallOutTransition	Shrinks an old screen towards center of the window and makes it transparent, revealing the new screen.
RiseInTransition	The exact opposite of FallOutTransition: grows the new screen from the center, overlapping and concealing an old one.

There's a small caveat in relation to setting these inside a .kv file: the transitions aren't imported by default, so you'll need to import the ones you want to use, using the following syntax (at the top of chat.kv):

```
#:import RiseInTransition kivy.uix.screenmanager.RiseInTransition
```

Now you can assign it to ScreenManager. Note that it's a Python class instantiation, so the parentheses at the end are required:

```
ScreenManager:
    transition: RiseInTransition()
```

Login screen layout

What happens inside the login screen, layout-wise, is very similar to the previous chapter's Sound recorder app: a GridLayout solves the task of aligning components on a grid.

The only thing that hasn't been used in this book yet is the TextInput widget. Kivy's text input behaves almost exactly like a button, with the obvious exception that you can type text into it. By default, TextInput is multiline, so we set the multiline property to False because multiline text inputs don't make much sense in the context of this app.

When running on a device with no physical keyboard attached, Kivy will fall back to a virtual onscreen keyboard, just as native apps do.

This is the code that implements the login screen layout (in the same Kivy language file, chat.kv, under ScreenManager):

```
Screen:
    name: 'login'

    BoxLayout:
        orientation: 'vertical'
```

```
GridLayout:
    Label:
        text: 'Server:'

    TextInput:
        id: server
        text: '127.0.0.1'

    Label:
        text: 'Nickname:'

    TextInput:
        id: nickname
        text: 'Kivy'

Button:
    text: 'Connect'
    on_press: root.current = 'chatroom'
```

Here, we add two text fields, `Server` and `Nickname`, with corresponding labels, and a **Connect** button. The event handler for the button has nothing to do with actual networking just yet and merely switches the screen to the chatroom, but this will change in the near future.

There is one interesting bit of styling needed to make a single-line `TextInput`. In addition to setting its `multiline` property to `False`, we want to align the text inside vertically in the middle (otherwise, it will stick to the top of the control, leaving a large gap at the bottom). We can achieve the proper alignment using the padding property like this:

```
<TextInput>:
    multiline: False
    padding: [10, 0.5 * (self.height - self.line_height)]
```

This `padding` line sets both left and right padding to 10, with top and bottom computed as *0.5 × (height of the widget − height of one line of text)*.

This is what the resulting screen looks like; it is pretty similar to other applications that we've produced during the course of this book.

Chat application's login screen

We could start writing code that connects to the server right now, but first let's get the primary screen, the chatroom, working. This will allow us to conduct meaningful tests right away afterwards.

Chatroom screen layout

Next on our list is the chatroom screen. It features a `ScrollView` widget for lengthy conversations, and since that's the first time a scrolling widget appears in this book, let's take a closer look at how it works.

The simplest `.kv` snippet to produce a scrolling widget is as follows:

```
<ChatLabel@Label>:
    text_size: (self.width, None)  # Step 1
    halign: 'left'
    valign: 'top'
    size_hint: (1, None)  # Step 2
    height: self.texture_size[1]  # Step 3

ScrollView:
    ChatLabel:
        text: 'Insert very long text with line\nbreaks'
```

If you add enough text to it so that it overflows the screen, it starts to scroll, similar to what you'd expect from a long list of items in iOS or Android.

This is how this layout works:

1. We constrain the `text_size` width (first value) of our custom `Label` subclass to the widget's available width, and let it choose the height depending on its contents by setting the second value to `None`.

2. Then, we set the vertical `size_hint` (second value) to `None` to force height of the widget to be computed independently of its container. Otherwise, it will be limited by the parent element, and thus there will be nothing to scroll.

3. Now, we can set the widget's height to be equal to the `texture_size` height (note that indexing is zero-based as usual, so the second value is indeed `texture_size[1]`). This will force the `ChatLabel` to become larger than the containing widget, `ScrollView`.

4. When the `ScrollView` detects that its child widget is larger than the available screen space, scrolling is enabled. It works as usual on mobile, and adds mouse wheel support on desktop.

Overscroll modes

You can also customize the overscroll effect of a `ScrollView` to mimic a behavior native to the corresponding platform (which still looks noticeably different from native components anyway, despite being similar in concept). At the time of writing, the Android-style edge glow isn't supported out of the box; the available options are listed as follows:

- `ScrollEffect`: This effect allows you to stop scrolling abruptly when you reach the end. This is similar to how desktop programs usually work, so this behavior might be desirable if the app in question is intended mostly for desktop.

- `DampedScrollEffect`: This is the default effect. It is similar to the bounce back effect found in iOS. This is arguably the best mode for mobile devices.

- `OpacityScrollEffect`: This effect is similar to `DampedScrollEffect` with added transparency when scrolling past the edge of the content.

To use one of these settings, import it from the `kivy.effects` module and assign to the `ScrollView.effect_cls` property, similar to the `ScreenManager` transitions just discussed. We aren't going to use this, as `DampedScrollEffect` suits our application just fine.

With all of these points in mind, this is what the chatroom screen layout looks like (in chat.kv):

```
Screen:
    name: 'chatroom'

    BoxLayout:
        orientation: 'vertical'

        Button:
            text: 'Disconnect'
            on_press: root.current = 'login'

        ScrollView:
            ChatLabel:
                id: chat_logs
                text: 'User says: foo\nUser says: bar'

        BoxLayout:
            height: 90
            orientation: 'horizontal'
            padding: 0
            size_hint: (1, None)

            TextInput:
                id: message

            Button:
                text: 'Send'
                size_hint: (0.3, 1)
```

The last line, size_hint, sets the horizontal proportion of the Button widget to 0.3, down from the default of 1. This makes the **Send** button smaller than the message input field.

In order to set the background of the messages area to white, we can use the following code:

```
<ScrollView>:
    canvas.before:
        Color:
            rgb: 1, 1, 1
        Rectangle:
            pos: self.pos
            size: self.size
```

This draws a white rectangle behind the `ScrollView` unconditionally before every other drawing operation takes place. Don't forget to tweak the `<ChatLabel>` class, setting text color to something readable on a light background:

```
#:import C kivy.utils.get_color_from_hex

<ChatLabel@Label>:
    color: C('#101010')
```

This is what we have so far:

Chatroom screen, devoid of meaningful conversations

Again, the **Disconnect** button just switches screens without any networking going on behind the scenes. This is the next topic actually; as you will see shortly, implementing simple network programs in Python is not very different in terms of complexity from building a simple user interface with Kivy.

Bringing the app online

This is the interesting part! We are going to establish the connection with the server, send and receive messages, and display meaningful output to users.

But first, let's take a look at the minimal, pure-Python implementation of the chat client, to see what's going on. This is low-level code using a socket to communicate. In practice, using a higher-level abstraction, like Twisted, is almost always advised; but if you're not familiar with the underlying concepts, it may be hard to grasp what happens in your code behind the scenes, which turns debugging into guesswork.

Building a simple Python client

In the following listing, we're reading user input from the console using the built-in `readline()` function and displaying the output with `print()`. This means that using this simple client is not vastly different from using Telnet—the UI consists of the exact same plain text in a terminal window—but this time we implement it ourselves from scratch using sockets.

We are going to need a number of Python modules, all from the standard library: `socket`, `sys` (for `sys.stdin`, standard input file descriptor), and the `select` module to implement efficient waiting until the data is available. Assuming a new file, let's call it `client.py`:

```
import select, socket, sys
```

This program doesn't need external dependencies at all; this is as pure-Python as it gets.

> Note than on Windows, `select` cannot poll file descriptors the same as sockets because of implementation details, so our code will not function correctly. Since this is only a demonstration of the low-level networking and not the final product, we aren't going to port it to marginal systems.

Now, we open the connection to server and do the usual CONNECT handshake:

```
s = socket.socket(socket.AF_INET, socket.SOCK_STREAM)
s.connect(('127.0.0.1', 9096))
s.send('CONNECT')
```

The next part in interesting: we wait for data to become available on either standard input (meaning that the user entered something), or the `s` socket (meaning that the server sent something our way). The waiting is achieved using the `select.select()` call:

```
rlist = (sys.stdin, s)
while 1:
    read, write, fail = select.select(rlist, (), ())
    for sock in read:
        if sock == s:  # receive message from server
            data = s.recv(4096)
            print(data)
        else:  # send message entered by user
            msg = sock.readline()
            s.send(msg)
```

Then, depending on the source of newly available data, we either print it on the screen in case of a message received from the server, or send it to the server if it's a message from the local user. Again, this is more or less what Telnet does, sans error checking.

As you can see, there is nothing inherently impossible or insanely complex in low-level networking. But for what it's worth, raw sockets are still quite cumbersome to handle and we will illustrate the high-level approach to the same code soon. However, this is what happens under the hood of any framework; ultimately, it's always sockets doing the heavy lifting, presented under a different sauce of abstractions (APIs).

> Note that in this tutorial we are not doing extensive error checking on purpose, because it will increase the amount of code by the factor of 2-3 and make it unwieldy.
>
> There are lots of things that can go wrong over the network; it's more fragile than it's commonly perceived to be. So if you're planning to compete with Skype *et al.*, be ready to do incredible amounts of error checking and testing: network problems such as packet loss and nationwide firewalls, to name a few, will surely bite at some point. No matter how well-planned your architecture is, making network services highly available is hard.

Kivy integration with Twisted

Another reason why our low-level client code is not a good fit for a Kivy application is that it relies on its own main loop (the `while 1:` part). It will take some work to make this code play well with the event loop that powers Kivy.

Instead, let's take advantage of the Twisted integration that's distributed as a part of Kivy. This also means that the same network library will be used on both the client and the server, making the code more uniform across the board.

The necessary step to make Kivy's main loop play well with Twisted is to run the following code before the Twisted framework is even imported:

```
from kivy.support import install_twisted_reactor
install_twisted_reactor()

from twisted.internet import reactor, protocol
```

The code should be at the very beginning of the `main.py` file. This is crucial to get right, otherwise everything will cease to function in obscure ways.

Now, let's implement the chat client using Twisted.

ChatClient and ChatClientFactory

On the Twisted part, there is surprisingly little to do, since the framework takes care of everything that's related to actual networking. These classes are used mostly to wire the "moving parts" of the program together.

The `ClientFactory` subclass, `ChatClientFactory`, will just store the Kivy app instance when initialized so that we can pass events to it later. Take a look at the following code:

```
class ChatClientFactory(protocol.ClientFactory):
    protocol = ChatClient

    def __init__(self, app):
        self.app = app
```

The complementary `ChatClient` class listens to `connectionMade` and `dataReceived` events from Twisted and passes them to the Kivy app:

```
class ChatClient(protocol.Protocol):
    def connectionMade(self):
        self.transport.write('CONNECT')
        self.factory.app.on_connect(self.transport)

    def dataReceived(self, data):
        self.factory.app.on_message(data)
```

Note the ubiquitous CONNECT handshake.

This is very different from the code utilizing raw sockets, right? At the same time, this is very similar to what happens on the server side in `server.py`. But, instead of actually handling events, we're just passing them to the `app` object.

UI integration

In order to finally see the whole picture, let's hook the networking code up to the UI and write the missing Kivy application class. The following are the cumulative updates that need to be applied to the `chat.kv` file:

```
Button:  # Connect button, found on login screen
    text: 'Connect'
    on_press: app.connect()

Button:  # Disconnect button, on chatroom screen
    text: 'Disconnect'
    on_press: app.disconnect()
```

```
TextInput:  # Message input, on chatroom screen
    id: message
    on_text_validate: app.send_msg()

Button:  # Message send button, on chatroom screen
    text: 'Send'
    on_press: app.send_msg()
```

Notice how buttons don't switch screens anymore, instead they call methods on app, similar to ChatClient event handling.

Having done that, we now need to implement a grand total of five methods that are missing from the Kivy application class: two for server-originated events that come from Twisted code (on_connect and on_message), and three more for the user interface events (connect, disconnect, and send_msg). This will make our Chat app actually usable.

Application logic of the client

Let's begin writing the program logic in roughly the lifecycle order: from connect() to disconnect().

In the connect() method, we pick up the values of **Server** and **Nickname** fields, as provided by the user. The nickname is then stored in self.nick, and the Twisted client connects to the specified host, as shown in the following code:

```
class ChatApp(App):
    def connect(self):
        host = self.root.ids.server.text
        self.nick = self.root.ids.nickname.text
        reactor.connectTCP(host, 9096,
                           ChatClientFactory(self))
```

Now, the ChatClient.connectionMade() function is called, passing control to the on_connect() method. We will use this event to store the connection in self.conn and switch screens. As discussed previously, buttons no longer switch screens directly; instead, we rely on more specific event handlers like this one:

```
# From here on these are methods of the ChatApp class
def on_connect(self, conn):
    self.conn = conn
    self.root.current = 'chatroom'
```

Now the main part: sending and receiving messages. This is very straightforward actually: to send a message we get the message text from the `TextInput`, get our nickname from `self.nick`, concatenate them together, and send the resulting line to the server. We also echo the same message onscreen and clear the message input box. The code is as follows:

```
def send_msg(self):
    msg = self.root.ids.message.text
    self.conn.write('%s:%s' % (self.nick, msg))
    self.root.ids.chat_logs.text += ('%s says: %s\n' %
                                     (self.nick, msg))
    self.root.ids.message.text = ''
```

Receiving messages is completely trivial; since we don't proactively keep track of them, just put the newly arrived message onscreen followed by a newline, and that's all:

```
def on_message(self, msg):
    self.root.ids.chat_logs.text += msg + '\n'
```

The last remaining method is `disconnect()`. It does exactly what it says on the tin: closes the connection and performs a general cleanup to return things back as they were when the program first started (notably, empties the `chat_logs` widget). Finally, it sends the user back to the login screen, so they can jump to another server or change nickname. The code is as follows:

```
def disconnect(self):
    if self.conn:
        self.conn.loseConnection()
        del self.conn
    self.root.current = 'login'
    self.root.ids.chat_logs.text = ''
```

With this, our app finally has the ability to send and receive chat messages.

Chat app in action

Caveats

During testing, the `server.py` script should obviously be running at all times; otherwise, our app won't have an endpoint to connect to. Presently, this will result in the app staying on the login screen; in the absence of an `on_connect()` call, the user won't get to the chatroom screen.

Also, when testing on Android, make sure you enter the correct IP address of the server, as it will *not* be `127.0.0.1` anymore — that's always the local machine, so on an Android device this will mean that very device and not the computer you're working on. Use the `ifconfig` utility (called `ipconfig` on Windows for additional confusion) to determine the correct network address of your machine.

Cross-application interoperability

One interesting property of the resulting application (besides the fact that it works at all) is that it's compatible with every client mentioned in this chapter. Users can connect to the server using Telnet, the pure-Python client, or the Kivy UI program — the core functionality is equally available to all of them.

This is very similar to how the Internet operates: once you have a well-defined protocol (such as HTTP), many unrelated parties can develop servers and clients that will be ultimately interoperable: web servers, web browsers, search engine crawlers, and so on.

A protocol is a higher form of an API, language- and system-independent, like a good foundation should be. While not many web developers are familiar with the API of, for example, Microsoft Silverlight released in 2007, anyone working in the field knows at least the basics of HTTP, documented in 1991. Such a level of ubiquity is nearly impossible to achieve with a library or framework.

Enhancements and eye candy

Now that our chat basically works, we can apply some finishing touches to it, for example, improve the chat log presentation. Since the client already displays anything that the server sends its way, we can easily use Kivy markup (**BBCode**-like markup language, discussed in *Chapter 1, Building a Clock App*) to style the conversation log.

To do this, let's assign a color to each user and then paint the nickname with this color and make it bold. This will help readability and generally look nicer than a wall of monochrome plain text.

We'll use the **Flat UI** color palette instead of generating purely random colors, because generating substantially different colors that look good when used together is by itself not an easy task.

Outgoing messages (those sent by the current user) don't come from the server and are added to chat log by the client code instead. So, we will paint the current user's nickname with a constant color right on the client.

After this update, the final code of the chat server, `server.py`, is as follows:

```
colors = ['7F8C8D', 'C0392B', '2C3E50', '8E44AD', '27AE60']

class Chat(protocol.Protocol):
    def connectionMade(self):
        self.color = colors.pop()
        colors.insert(0, self.color)
```

Given a finite list of colors, we pop one from the end of the list, and then insert it back to the front, creating a rotating buffer.

> If you're familiar with the more advanced `itertools` module from the standard library, you can rewrite the code we just saw like this:
>
> ```
> import itertools
> colors = itertools.cycle(('7F8C8D', 'C0392B',
> '2C3E50', '8E44AD', '27AE60'))
> def connectionMade(self):
>     self.color = colors.next()
>     # next(colors) in Python 3
> ```

And now, we will discuss the bit where we pass the message to the client. The markup for the desired effect is very straightforward: `[b][color]Nickname[/color][/b]`. The code that makes use of it is equally simple:

```
for t in transports:
    if t is not self.transport:
        t.write('[b][color={}]{}:[/color][/b] {}'
                .format(self.color, user, msg))
```

The client in `main.py` is also updated to match formatting, as discussed earlier. Here, we have a constant color, which is different from the ones assigned by the server, so that the current user always stands out. The code is as follows:

```
def send_msg(self):
    msg = self.root.ids.message.text
```

```
self.conn.write('%s:%s' % (self.nick, msg))
self.root.ids.chat_logs.text += (
    '[b][color=2980B9]{}:[/color][/b] {}\n'
    .format(self.nick, msg))
```

Then, we set the `markup` property to `True` on the conversation log widget, `ChatLabel`, as shown in the following code snippet, and we're (almost) done:

```
<ChatLabel@Label>:
    markup: True
```

However, before we solve a problem with this approach (and there's indeed at least one serious problem here), here's the obligatory resulting screenshot. This is how the final conversation screen looks like:

Colorful chat logs help readability and generally
look better and more "polished"

Escaping the special syntax

One shortcoming in this code, as mentioned earlier, is that now we have special syntax in the protocol that's interpreted in a certain way on the client. Users can forge (or just inadvertently use, by pure chance) the BBCode-ish markup, creating unwanted visual glitches, such as assigning very large font sizes and unreadable colors. For example, if one of the users posts an unclosed `[i]` tag, all following text in the chatroom will be italicized. That's pretty bad.

In order to prevent users from highlighting text in random ways, we need to escape all markup that may exist in the message. Fortunately, Kivy provides a function to do just that, `kivy.utils.escape_markup`. Bad news is that it's been bugged since 2012.

There's a high probability that the function will have been fixed by the time you're reading this book, but for the sake of completeness, here's an implementation that works:

```
def esc_markup(msg):
    return (msg.replace('&', '&amp;')
               .replace('[', '&bl;')
               .replace(']', '&br;'))
```

With this, all characters that are special to Kivy markup are replaced with HTML-style character entities, so the markup passed through this function will be displayed as is and won't affect the rich text attributes in any way.

We need to call this function in two places, on the server when sending messages to clients, and on the client when displaying messages from self (the current user).

In `server.py`, the relevant portion of the code looks like this:

```
t.write('[b][color={}]{}:[/color][/b] {}'
        .format(self.color, user,
                esc_markup(msg)))
```

In `main.py`, the implementation is similar:

```
self.root.ids.chat_logs.text += (
    '[b][color=2980B9]{}:[/color][/b] {}\n'
    .format(self.nick, esc_markup(msg)))
```

Here, the vulnerability is patched; now users can safely send BBCode markup to each other if they choose to do so.

Interestingly, this type of bug is also very pervasive in Internet apps. When applied to websites, it's called **cross-site scripting** (**XSS**) and allows much more damage than merely changing fonts and colors.

Don't forget to sanitize all user input in all scenarios that may involve commands (such as markup, inline scripts, even ANSI escape codes) mixed in with the data; neglecting to do so is a sure-fire disaster waiting to happen.

What's next

Obviously, this is only the beginning. The implementation at hand still has a vast number of deficiencies: user names aren't enforced to be unique, and there is no history and no support for fetching messages that have been sent while other parties were offline. Hence, bad network with frequent disconnects will render this application mostly unusable.

But what matters is that these points can certainly be addressed, and we already have a working prototype. In the start-up world, having a prototype is an attractive quality, particularly when raising funds; if you're programming for fun mostly, it's even more so, as seeing a working product is greatly motivating (as opposed to observing a pile of code that doesn't so much as run yet).

Summary

As we saw in this chapter, client-server application development (and generally speaking, networking on the application level) isn't necessarily inherently complex. Even the low-level code utilizing sockets is quite manageable.

There are, of course, many gray areas and aspects that are hard to get right when writing an app that makes heavy use of the network. Examples of these include working around high latency, restoring an interrupted connection, and syncing across a large number of nodes (especially peer-to-peer or multi-master, when none of the machines have the full dataset).

Another relatively new class of network problems is the political one. Lately, Internet regulations are being implemented by governments of varying oppressiveness, ranging from relatively logical (for example, blocking resources promoting terrorism) to completely nonsensical (for example, banning educational sites like Wikipedia, major news sites, or video games). This type of connectivity problem is also known for high collateral damage, for example, if a **content delivery network** (**CDN**) goes down, then many sites that link to it will cease to work properly.

However, with careful programming and testing, it is certainly possible to overcome every obstacle and deliver a product of exceptional quality to your users. Rich Python infrastructure shoulders some of this burden for you, as shown in our Chat program: many low-level details are abstracted with the help of Kivy and Twisted, two excellent Python libraries.

The possibilities in this field, given the universal accessibility, are nothing short of endless. We will discuss and implement a way more interesting use case for a networked app in the next chapter, so read on.

5
Making a Remote Desktop App

To summarize the networking theme started in the previous chapter, let's build another client-server application—a Remote Desktop app. This time our app will solve a more complex practical task and communicate using a "real" application-level protocol.

Let's discuss the task at hand for a moment. First, the purpose: a typical remote desktop program allows users to access other computers remotely via local area network or the Internet. It is common to use such apps for ad hoc technical support or remote assistance, for example, by IT personnel in a big company.

Second, the terminology: the *host* machine is the one being remotely controlled (running the remote-control server), and the *client* is the system that controls the host. Remote system management is basically the process of user interaction with the host machine using another computer system (client) as a proxy.

So, this whole endeavor boils down to the following activities:

- Collect relevant user input (such as mouse and keyboard events) on the client and apply it to the host
- Send any relevant output (most commonly a screen capture, sometimes audio, and so on) from the host machine back to the client

These two steps are performed repeatedly until the session ends and the connection between machines is closed.

The definition that we discussed earlier is very broad and many commercial packages compete on feature completeness, some even allow you to play video games remotely—with accelerated graphics and gaming controller input. We are going to limit the scope of our work so that the project can be completed within a reasonable time:

- For the user input, only clicks (or taps, there is no difference in this context) are accepted and sent over.

- For the output, just the screen capture is taken, because capturing sound and streaming it over the network can be way too challenging for a tutorial.

- Only Windows hosts are supported. Any recent Windows version should be fine; Windows 7 or later is recommended. We assume desktop and not WinRT or Windows Phone. There are no such restrictions on the client, as it runs a portable Kivy app.

The last point is unfortunate, but since every system uses different APIs to take screenshots and emulate clicks, we should start with the most popular one anyway. Support for other host systems can be added to the server later; this isn't overly complex *per se*, just very platform-specific.

Regarding the OS choice: if you don't use the Windows OS, no worries. This is the same as with Android earlier: you can easily run Windows inside a virtual machine. VirtualBox VM is a go-to solution for desktop virtualization, and it is freely available from the official website at `https://www.virtualbox.org/`.

On a Mac, Parallels is a better option in terms of usability and the operating system integration. The only possible downside is its hefty price tag.

In this chapter, we will cover the following topics of interest:

- Writing an HTTP server in Python with the help of the Flask microframework

- Taking screenshots using the **Python Imaging Library** (**PIL**)

- Emulating clicks on Windows, utilizing the WinAPI functionality

- Prototyping a simple JavaScript client and using it for testing

- Finally, building a Kivy-based HTTP client app for our remote desktop server

The server

To simplify testing and possible future integration, we want to make our server talk a well-established application-level protocol this time. Let's use **Hypertext Transfer Protocol (HTTP)**; in addition to relative simplicity and ease of testing, it has at least two more valuable qualities:

- Abundance of libraries to support it, both server- and client-side. This is obviously a consequence of HTTP powering the Internet, the largest and most popular network to date.

- Unlike many other protocols, for HTTP we can write a very simple proof-of-concept JavaScript client that runs inside a web browser. This isn't strictly related to the topic of the book, but may prove useful in a number of scenarios, especially when debugging.

The library of choice that we'll utilize to build the server is Flask. There is another popular Python web framework, Django, that's also highly recommended. However, Django projects generally end up being more heavyweight, so we'll stick with Flask for this simplistic server.

To install Flask on the server, the following command is sufficient:

```
pip install Flask
```

If you don't have `pip` installed, try running the `easy_install pip` command first. Depending on your Python setup, you may need to run this from a privileged user having sufficient permissions.

On Windows, Python setup tends to be much more convoluted compared to Mac OS or Linux; please see the previous chapter for more extensive details on Python package management. Alternatively, you could jump straight to the official pip reference, found at `https://pip.pypa.io/en/latest/installing.html`. This document covers the installation of `pip` across all supported operating systems.

Note that, similar to the previous project we built (the Chat application from the previous chapter), Kivy framework doesn't have to be installed on the server. Our server-side code runs headless, without any user interface whatsoever—other than perhaps an occasional console output.

The Flask web server

A web server is usually structured as a series of handlers bound to different URLs. Such binding is commonly called *routing*. The goal of Flask, among the others, is to obviate this binding and make it easy to add new routes to a program.

The simplest, one-page Flask server (let's name it `server.py`) goes like this:

```python
from flask import Flask
app = Flask(__name__)

@app.route('/')
def index():
    return 'Hello, Flask'

if __name__ == '__main__':
    app.run(host='0.0.0.0', port=7080, debug=True)
```

In Flask, routing is designated with decorators such as `@app.route('/')`, which is perfect when you only have a small number of distinct URLs.

The `'/'` route is the server root; this is the default when you type a domain name into address bar. To open the trivial website we just wrote in your browser, just go to http://127.0.0.1:7080 on the same machine (don't forget to start the server first). When you do that, a **Hello, Flask** message should appear, confirming that our toy HTTP server works.

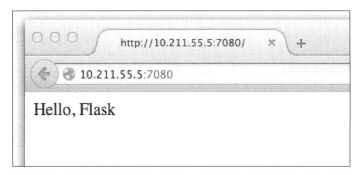

A minimalistic website powered by Flask

Those not familiar with web servers may wonder about the strange argument to `app.run()`, the **0.0.0.0** IP address. That's not a valid IP address that you can connect to, as it doesn't designate a network interface by itself (it is non-routable). In the context of a server, binding to this IP usually means that we want our app to listen on all IPv4 network interfaces—that is, respond to requests from all the available IP addresses that the machine has.

This is different from the default, localhost (or 127.0.0.1) setting: listening exclusively on the localhost IP allows connections from the same machine alone, therefore, this mode of operation can be helpful for debugging or testing. In this example, however, we use a more production-oriented setting, 0.0.0.0 — this makes the machine accessible from the outside world (typically, the local area network). Note that this doesn't automatically bypass the router; it should work for your LAN, but may need additional configuration to be accessible globally.

Also, don't forget to allow the server through the firewall, as it takes precedence over application-level settings.

Choice of port

The port number by itself doesn't make much sense; what matters is that you use the same number in both server and client, be it a web browser or a Kivy app.

Be aware that on almost all systems, ports below 1024 can only be opened by a privileged user account (root or Administrator). Many ports in that range are already assigned to existing services anyway, so it's not advised to pick port numbers under 1024 for the specific needs of your application.

The default port for the HTTP protocol is 80, for example, `http://www.w3.org/` is the same as `http://www.w3.org:80/`, and usually you don't need to specify it.

You might notice that web development in Python is very easy — a Python script just a couple of lines long can get you up and running with a dynamic web server. Expectedly, not everything is this simple; some things aren't immediately available in the form of reusable library.

This can be viewed as a competitive advantage, by the way: if you're struggling with implementation of a non-trivial bit of functionality, chances are that not many instances of this thing exist, if at all, which makes your product more unique and competitive in the end.

Advanced server functionality – taking screenshots

Once we have decided on a protocol and a server-side toolkit, our next challenges involve taking screenshots and simulating clicks that come from the client. Just a quick reminder: in this section, we will be covering only a Windows-specific implementation; adding Mac and Linux support is left as an exercise for the reader.

Luckily, the PIL has just the function we need; by calling `PIL.ImageGrab.grab()`, we get a screenshot of our Windows desktop as an RGB bitmap. All that's left is hooking it up to Flask so that the screenshot is properly served over HTTP.

We will use a fork of an old and basically unmaintained PIL module called **Pillow**. By the way, Pillow is a great open source project used by many developers; if you're looking to contribute to Python userland, look no further. A good starting point will be the official Pillow documentation at `http://pillow.readthedocs.org/`.

Install the library exactly like you installed Flask:

```
pip install Pillow
```

Pillow comes with binaries for Windows pre-packaged, so you don't need a compiler or a Visual Studio installed on your machine.

Now we're good to go. The following code demonstrates how to serve screenshots (or any other PIL bitmaps for that matter) from a Flask server:

```
from flask import send_file
from PIL import ImageGrab
from StringIO import StringIO

@app.route('/desktop.jpeg')
def desktop():
    screen = ImageGrab.grab()
    buf = StringIO()
    screen.save(buf, 'JPEG', quality=75)
    buf.seek(0)
    return send_file(buf, mimetype='image/jpeg')
```

If you're not familiar with `StringIO`, it's a file-like object that is stored in memory and not written to disk. Such "virtual files" are useful when we need to use an API that expects a file object on a vanity data. In this example, we don't want to store a screenshot, which is temporary and not reusable by definition, in a physical file. The sheer overhead of continuously dumping data on disk isn't justified; it's usually much better (and way faster) to allocate a chunk of memory and immediately free it when the response is sent.

The rest of the code should be self-evident. We're getting a `screen` picture from a `PIL.ImageGrab.grab()` call, saving it using `screen.save()` to a lossy, low-quality JPEG file to save bandwidth, and finally sending the image to user with the MIME type of `'image/jpeg'`, so that it will be immediately recognized by web browsers as a picture of the correct type.

In this situation, as in many others, low quality is actually a desirable property of the system; we're optimizing for throughput and round-trip speed, not for visual quality of each individual frame in a series.

The same goes for the connotation of low-quality code: it's actually great to be able to produce a quick and dirty prototype sometimes, for example, when fiddling with a new concept or doing market research.

Though it seems strange at first, the `buf.seek(0)` call is needed to *rewind* the `StringIO` instance; otherwise, it's at the end of the data stream and won't yield anything to `send_file()`.

Now you can test the server implementation that we have so far by pointing your browser of choice at `http://127.0.0.1:7080/desktop.jpeg` and taking a peek on the Windows desktop of the machine where the `server.py` script is running. If the code works correctly, it should produce a picture as displayed in the following screenshot:

Windows desktop, as seen by the Flask server (fragment)

An interesting part here is the route, **"desktop.jpeg"**. Naming URLs after files became somewhat customary because ancient web server tools like **Personal Home Page** (**PHP**), a toy programming language suitable for building simple dynamic sites, operated on physical files. This means that there was basically no concept of routing—you could just enter the name of the script in an address bar to run it on the server.

Obviously, this created gaping chasms in the web server security, including (but not limited to) remotely viewing system configuration files by entering, for example, `'/../../etc/passwd'` in place of a URL, and being able to upload and run malicious scripts serving as Trojans (backdoors) that are used to eventually seize control of the server.

Python web frameworks have mostly learned this lesson. While you can try and replicate such an insecure setup using Python, it is both non-trivial to do and strongly discouraged. Additionally, Python libraries usually don't come bundled with bad PHP-style configurations by default.

Today, serving actual files directly from the filesystem isn't unheard of, but is used mostly for static files. Still, we sometimes name dynamic routes as if they were files (`/index.html`, `/desktop.jpeg`, and so on) to convey the semantics of what kind of content users should expect from such URLs.

Emulating clicks

With the screenshots part finished, the last non-trivial bit of functionality that we need to implement on the server is click emulation. For this we won't use an external library; we'll employ WinAPI (the underlying programming interface that powers, directly or indirectly, all Windows apps) instead, using the built-in Python `ctypes` module.

But first we need to get the click coordinates from the URL. Let's use regular GET parameters that look like this: `/click?x=100&y=200`. This should be trivial to manually test in a browser, as opposed to POST and other HTTP methods that may require additional software to emulate.

A parser for simple URL arguments is built into Flask, and they can be accessed as shown in the next code snippet:

```
from flask import request

@app.route('/click')
def click():
    try:
        x = int(request.args.get('x'))
        y = int(request.args.get('y'))
    except TypeError:
        return 'error: expecting 2 ints, x and y'
```

Error handling here, of all places, is recommended when prototyping, because it's very easy to forget or send malformed parameters, so we're checking for just that— the (in)ability to get numbers from GET request args. Responding with an obvious error message also helps debugging when (or if) you see this message, as it's completely obvious what's going on and where to look for the problem—in the code that passed arguments to `/click`.

After we have the coordinates for a click, an invocation of WinAPI is in order. We need two functions, both residing in `user32.dll`: the `SetCursorPos()` that moves the mouse pointer, and the `mouse_event()` that simulates a number of mouse-related events, for example, the mouse button being pressed or released.

> By the way, the `32` part in `user32.dll` isn't related to your system being 32- or 64-bit. The Win32 API first appeared in Windows NT, it predates the AMD64 (x86_64) architecture by at least 7 years and is called Win32 as opposed to an older, 16-bit WinAPI.

The first argument to `mouse_event()` is an event type, which is a C enum (in other words, a set of integer constants). Let's define these constants in our Python code for the sake of readability, as using literal 2 for **mouse down** and 4 for **mouse up** isn't very readable. This amounts to the following lines:

```python
import ctypes
user32 = ctypes.windll.user32  # this is the user32.dll reference

MOUSEEVENTF_LEFTDOWN = 2
MOUSEEVENTF_LEFTUP = 4
```

> For the full reference on WinAPI functions and constants, please visit the **Microsoft Developer Network (MSDN)** site, or more specifically the following:
>
> - `SetCursorPos()`: http://msdn.microsoft.com/en-us/library/windows/desktop/ms648394%28v=vs.85%29.aspx
> - `mouse_event()`: http://msdn.microsoft.com/en-us/library/windows/desktop/ms646260%28v=vs.85%29.aspx
>
> It isn't feasible to reproduce this content here due to its size, and we won't use most of the available functionality anyway; WinAPI is all-encompassing and does more or less everything, usually in more than one way.

This is the fun part: we get to actually emulate clicks. (The first part of the function, where x and y are fetched from GET parameters, is unchanged.) The code is as follows:

```python
@app.route('/click')
def click():
    try:
```

```
        x = int(request.args.get('x'))
        y = int(request.args.get('y'))
    except:
        return 'error'

    user32.SetCursorPos(x, y)
    user32.mouse_event(MOUSEEVENTF_LEFTDOWN, 0, 0, 0, 0)
    user32.mouse_event(MOUSEEVENTF_LEFTUP, 0, 0, 0, 0)
    return 'done'
```

This does just what it says if you try reading the code aloud: the function moves the mouse to the desired position and then simulates the left mouse button click (with button press and release being two separate actions).

Now, you should be able to manually control the mouse cursor on the host machine. Try visiting a URL such as `http://127.0.0.1:7080/click?x=10&y=10` and make sure there is something in the top-left corner of the screen. You'll notice how that item gets selected.

You can even perform a double-click if you refresh the page sufficiently fast. This may require that you run the browser on another machine; don't forget to substitute the real host IP instead of `127.0.0.1`.

JavaScript client

In this section, we will briefly cover the development of a JavaScript remote desktop client mockup, which is feasible mostly because we use the HTTP protocol. This uncomplicated client will run in the browser and serve as a prototype of the Kivy remote desktop application that we're going to build next.

If you aren't familiar with JavaScript, don't worry; the language is very easy to get into and may even look similar to Python, depending on code style. We are also going to use **jQuery** for heavy lifting, such as DOM operations and AJAX calls.

 In a production setting, jQuery usage may be frowned upon (and rightfully so), especially when aiming for a lean, high-performance codebase. However, for quick prototyping or vanity web apps, jQuery shines because it facilitates writing functioning, albeit suboptimal, code very quickly.

For a web app, we need to serve a complete HTML page instead of just **Hello, Flask**. To do this, let's create the `index.html` file that resides in a folder named `static`, where Flask expects to find it:

```html
<!DOCTYPE html>
<html>
    <head>
        <meta charset="UTF-8">
        <title>Remote Desktop</title>
    </head>
    <body>
        <script src="//code.jquery.com/jquery-1.11.1.js"></script>
        <script>
            // code goes here
        </script>
    </body>
</html>
```

The preceding listing is a very basic HTML5 document. It does nothing special at the moment: jQuery is loaded from the official CDN, but that's it—no moving parts yet.

To serve this new file from Flask, replace the `index()` function in `server.py` with the following code:

```python
@app.route('/')
def index():
    return app.send_static_file('index.html')
```

This works just like the `desktop()` function earlier, but reads a real file from disk this time.

Endless loop of screenshots

To start off, let's display a continuous screencast: our script is going to request a new screenshot every two seconds, and then show it to the user immediately. Since we're writing a web app, all complex stuff is actually handled by the browser: an `<img>` tag loads an image and displays it on the screen, with very little effort on our part.

Here is the algorithm for this functionality:

1. Remove the old `<img>` tag (if any)

2. Add a new `<img>` tag

3. Repeat after 2 seconds

In JavaScript, this can be implemented as follows:

```
function reload_desktop() {
    $('img').remove()
    $('<img>', {src: '/desktop.jpeg?' +
            Date.now()}).appendTo('body')
}

setInterval(reload_desktop, 2000)
```

There are two things here that may need some additional insight:

- The `$()` jQuery function selects elements on the page so that we can perform various operations on them, such as `.remove()` or `.insert()`.

- `Date.now()` returns the current timestamp, namely, the number of milliseconds since January 1, 1970. We use this number to prevent caching. It will be different on every invocation; so when appended to the (otherwise constant) `/desktop.jpeg` URL, timestamp will make it unique, as far as the web browser is concerned.

Let's also downscale the image so that it doesn't exceed our browser window's width and remove any margins. This is also very simple to achieve; just add this small stylesheet in the `<head>` section of the HTML document:

```
<style>
    body { margin: 0 }
    img { max-width: 100% }
</style>
```

Try resizing the browser window and notice how the image shrinks to fit.

Remote desktop viewed in the browser, scaled to the size of the browser window

You may also notice that the image flickers when reloading. This happens because we show `desktop.jpeg` to the user immediately, before it is fully loaded. Even more problematic than visual glitches is the fixed time frame for download, which we arbitrarily chose to be two seconds. In the case of slow network connections, users won't be able to complete the download and see the whole picture of their desktop.

We are going to address these problems in the Kivy implementation of the remote desktop client.

Passing clicks to host

This is the more interesting part: we are going to capture clicks on the `<img>` element and pass them to the server. This is achieved using `.bind()` on (counterintuitively) the `<body>` element. This is because we're constantly adding and removing the image, so any events that are bound to an image instance will be lost after the next refresh (and constantly rebinding them is just unnecessarily repetitive and wrong). The code listing is as follows:

```
function send_click(event) {
    var fac = this.naturalWidth / this.width
    $.get('/click', {x: 0|fac * event.clientX,
                     y: 0|fac * event.clientY})
}

$('body').on('click', 'img', send_click)
```

In this code, we're calculating the "real" click coordinates first: the image may be shrunk to fit browser width, so we compute the ratio and multiply click position by that:

$$x, y_{server} = \frac{width_{natural}}{width_{scaled}} \times x, y_{client}$$

The `0|expression` syntax in JavaScript is a superior alternative to `Math.floor()`, as it is both faster and more concise. There are minor semantic differences too, but they aren't important at this point (if at all).

Now, utilizing the jQuery `$.get()` helper function, we send the result of the previous computation to the server. There is no processing of the server's response, since we're going to display a new screenshot in a moment anyway—if there was any effect to our last action, it will be reflected visually.

Using this trivial remote desktop client, we're already able to view the screen of the remote host, launch and control programs running on that machine. Now, let's re-implement this prototype in Kivy while improving it along the way, in particular, making it more suitable for use on mobile devices, adding scrolling and removing flicker.

Kivy Remote Desktop app

It's time to build a fully functional remote desktop client using Kivy. There are several things that we can reuse from the previous app, the Chat app from *Chapter 4, Kivy Networking*. Conceptually, these apps are quite similar: they consist of two screens each, with one screen resembling a login form with server IP address. Let's capitalize on this similarity and reuse parts of the chat.kv file in our brand new remotedesktop.kv, in particular, the ScreenManager setup that is practically unchanged.

The login form

The following listing defines the login form. It is composed of three elements—field caption, input field itself, and a login button—positioned in a row at the top of the screen:

```
Screen:
    name: 'login'

    BoxLayout:
        orientation: 'horizontal'
        y: root.height - self.height

        Label:
            text: 'Server IP:'
            size_hint: (0.4, 1)

        TextInput:
            id: server
            text: '10.211.55.5'  # put your server IP here

        Button:
            text: 'Connect'
            on_press: app.connect()
            size_hint: (0.4, 1)
```

There is just one input field this time, **Server IP**. In fact, you can also enter the hostname if it's resolvable from the given machine, but let's stick to this naming as it is less ambiguous. A LAN may not have a DNS server, or it may be configured in a way that does not match users' expectations about hostnames.

The simple and unambiguous login form

It's not that IP addresses are very user-friendly, but we don't have many options here—building an autodiscovery network service to avoid this, while very much desirable in real-world scenarios, can also be very convoluted (and probably deserves its own book anyway due to the sheer number of available techniques and possible caveats).

You need to understand basic networking in order to address machines in complex scenarios such as connecting to a machine sitting behind router. As mentioned earlier, this is pretty much out of the scope of this work, but here are some quick tips:

- It's considerably easier to test network apps when all of your machines are sitting in the same network (are connected to the same router, from the same side of the router topologically).
- Taking the previous point to the extreme means running every test box inside a VM on the same physical machine. This way, you can emulate any network topology you want, without the hassle of rearranging physical wires every time you want to tweak something.
- To see every IP address assigned to every network interface of a computer, run `ifconfig` (on a Mac or Linux machine) or `ipconfig` (Windows). Usually, your external (Internet) IP is not among those displayed in the output, but your local (LAN) network address is.

There isn't much else to say about the login screen, as it consists entirely of building blocks that we've already discussed during the course of this book. Let's move on to the second screen, and ultimately to the source code powering the client-server engine.

The remote desktop screen

This is the second and last screen in our application, the remote desktop screen. It will be scrollable in two dimensions, given a big enough screen size on the host machine. Since full HD (1080p and more) resolutions aren't uncommon in today's mobile devices, let alone desktop computers, it may so happen that we won't need any scrolling at all.

We can build a scrolling layout based on a similar principle as the chatroom pane from the Chat app that we've built in *Chapter 4, Kivy Networking*. As said earlier, the scrolling will be two-dimensional; an additional difference is that we don't want any overscroll (bounce back) effects this time to avoid unnecessary confusion. We are presenting a (remote) desktop to the user, and the operating system's desktop usually doesn't have this feature.

The `remotedesktop.kv` code behind this screen is actually very concise. Let's examine how different parts of it contribute to the task at hand:

```
Screen:
    name: 'desktop'

    ScrollView:
        effect_cls: ScrollEffect

        Image:
            id: desktop
            nocache: True
            on_touch_down: app.send_click(args[1])
            size: self.texture_size
            size_hint: (None, None)
```

To make scrolling work, we combine `ScrollView` with `Image`, which may become larger than the available screen space.

On `ScrollView`, we set `effect_cls: ScrollEffect` to disable overscroll; if you would like to leave the overscroll behavior intact, just remove this line. Since the `ScrollEffect` name isn't imported by default, we'll have to import it:

```
#:import ScrollEffect kivy.effects.scroll.ScrollEffect
```

Setting the `size_hint` property of `Image` to `(None, None)` is crucial; otherwise, Kivy will scale the image to fit, which isn't desirable in this case. The `size_hint` property set to `None` means *let me set the size manually*.

Then, we do just that, binding the `size` property to `self.texture_size`. With this setting, the image will be of the same size as a `desktop.jpeg` texture provided by the server (it depends on the host machine's physical desktop size, obviously, so we cannot hard-code it).

There is also the `nocache: True` property that instructs Kivy to never cache the desktop image that is temporary by definition.

Last but not least, an interesting property of `Image` is its `on_touch_down` handler. This time, we want to pass the exact coordinates and other properties of the touch event, and that's exactly what `args[1]` means. In case you're wondering, `args[0]` is the widget being clicked; in this case that's the image itself (we have just one `Image` instance, so there's no need to pass it to the event handler).

Loop of screenshots in Kivy

Now we're going to assemble everything together in Python. As opposed to the JavaScript implementation, we don't get the image loading and related functionality entirely for free, so there will be a bit more code; still, it's pretty easy to implement these, while maintaining better control over the whole process, as you will see shortly.

In order to load images asynchronously, we're going to use the Kivy built-in class called `Loader`, from the `kivy.loader` module. The program flow will go like this:

1. When a user clicks or taps on **Connect** on the login screen after filling the **Server IP** field, the `RemoteDesktopApp.connect()` function is invoked.
2. It passes control to `reload_desktop()`, the function that starts the image download from the `/desktop.jpeg` endpoint.
3. When the image is loaded, `Loader` invokes `desktop_loaded()`, which puts the image on the screen and schedules the next call of `reload_desktop()`. Thus, we get an asynchronous endless loop retrieving screenshots from the host system.

The image is put on the screen *after* it was successfully loaded, so there will be no flickering this time like there was in the JavaScript prototype. (It's solvable in JS too, certainly, but that's not the goal of this write-up.)

Let's take a closer look at the aforementioned functions in `main.py`:

```
from kivy.loader import Loader

class RemoteDesktopApp(App):
    def connect(self):
        self.url = ('http://%s:7080/desktop.jpeg' %
```

```
                        self.root.ids.server.text)
        self.send_url = ('http://%s:7080/click?' %
                         self.root.ids.server.text)
        self.reload_desktop()
```

We save `url` (the full location of `/desktop.jpeg` together with the server IP) and `send_url` (the location of `/click` endpoint to pass clicks to host), and then pass the execution to the `RemoteDesktopApp.reload_desktop()` function, which is also very brief:

```
def reload_desktop(self, *args):
    desktop = Loader.image(self.url, nocache=True)
    desktop.bind(on_load=self.desktop_loaded)
```

In the preceding function, we start downloading the image. When it's complete, the freshly loaded image will be passed on to `RemoteDesktopApp.desktop_loaded()`.

Don't forget to disable the default aggressive caching by passing the `nocache=True` argument. Omitting this step will result in the `desktop.jpeg` image loading only once, because its URL stays the same. In JavaScript, we solved the same problem by appending `?timestamp` to the URL to make it unique, and we could certainly mimic such behavior in Python, but that's a hack. Kivy's way of specifying `nocache` is cleaner and more readable.

Here, you can observe the culmination of the image downloading procedure:

```
from kivy.clock import Clock

def desktop_loaded(self, desktop):
    if desktop.image.texture:
        self.root.ids.desktop.texture = \
            desktop.image.texture

    Clock.schedule_once(self.reload_desktop, 1)

    if self.root.current == 'login':
        self.root.current = 'desktop'
```

This function receives the new image, `desktop`. Then, we proceed to replace the texture on screen with the freshly loaded one and schedule the next iteration of the screenshot loop to occur in a second.

The `Clock` object was discussed briefly in our first project (*Chapter 1, Building a Clock App*). There, we used it to perform periodical actions by calling `schedule_interval()`, similar to `setInterval()` in JavaScript; in this case, we want a one-time invocation, `schedule_once()`, along the lines of `setTimeout()` in JS.

Now, it is time to switch screens from login to the remote desktop screen. The following screenshot summarizes what we have so far:

A read-only (still unable to pass clicks back to host) Remote Desktop app

Sending clicks

The remote desktop viewer is ready and features scrolling and instant transition between frames (no flickering whatsoever). There is one last thing left to implement: sending clicks to host. For this, we will listen to the `on_touch_down` event on the image and pass the coordinates of touches to an event handler function, `send_click()`.

This is where it happens in `remotedesktop.kv`:

```
Screen:
    name: 'desktop'

    ScrollView:
        effect_cls: ScrollEffect

        Image:
            on_touch_down: app.send_click(args[1])
            # The rest of the properties unchanged
```

To put it in context, here is the Python counterpart in `class RemoteDesktopApp`:

```
def send_click(self, event):
    params = {'x': int(event.x),
              'y': int(self.root.ids.desktop.size[1] -
                       event.y)}
    urlopen(self.send_url + urlencode(params))
```

We gather the click coordinates and feed them to the server via HTTP GET request using the network-related functions from the Python's standard library.

One major caveat here is the coordinate system: in Kivy, the y axis is upwards, while it's usually downwards in Windows and elsewhere (for example, in browsers). To fix this, we subtract `event.y` from the desktop height.

Another slightly less problematic aspect is the use of Python's standard library across different Python versions: the `urllib` [2] module's structure was changed significantly in transition from Python 2 to Python 3.

To account for these changes, we can use the following way of doing imports:

```
try:  # python 2
    from urllib import urlencode
except ImportError:  # python 3
    from urllib.parse import urlencode

try:  # python 2
    from urllib2 import urlopen
except ImportError:  # python 3
    from urllib.request import urlopen
```

While not strikingly beautiful, this approach should help you with the Python upgrade, should you attempt it. (Targeting a fixed version of Python is also perfectly acceptable, by the way. In fact, many companies do just that at the time of this writing, including the very employer of Guido van Rossum, creator of the Python programming language.)

 In this case, the Python standard library is perfectly fine; however, if at any time you find yourself writing repetitive, boring, and unimaginative HTTP-related code, consider using an excellent **Requests** library by Kenneth Reitz instead. Visit `http://python-requests.org/` for more information and examples. It's pretty amazing how concise and to the point its syntax is. Wholeheartedly recommended, this library is a work of art.

What's next

Now, you have a Remote Desktop app that mostly works as intended, especially over LAN or a fast Internet connection. As usual, there are many additional problems to solve and a lot of new features to implement if you're interested and willing to tackle with this topic some more:

- Send mouse movement as a separate event. This may also apply to double clicks, drag and drop, and so on.

- Try to account for network latency. If the user is on a slow connection, you can turn image quality further down on the server to compensate. Providing the user with a visual clue that something is happening in the background also helps.

- Make the server cross-platform so that it runs on a Mac, Linux, and maybe even Android and Chrome OS.

Also, remember that this is an industry-strong task. It is objectively hard to build such software, let alone make it flawless and blazing fast. Kivy helps a great deal on the UI side of things, facilitates image downloading and caching, but that's it.

So, don't worry if something doesn't work immediately as you implement it—trial and error is not at all uncommon in this case. At times, you just need to keep putting one foot in front of the other.

There is much to learn in the field of networking, and engineers knowledgeable in this field are few and valued highly, so it certainly pays off to dig into the topic of computers communicating with other computers.

Summary

This constitutes the Remote Desktop app walkthrough. The resulting application can be actually used for simple tasks, for example, occasionally clicking on the **Play** button in iTunes or closing a program. More demanding interactions, in particular administrative tasks, may require much more complex software.

We also built a Flask-powered web server capable of dynamically producing images and interacting with the host system. On top of it, we launched a "light" JavaScript version of the app featuring pretty much the same functionality. The morale of this story is that our Kivy app does not exist in isolation. Far from it, in fact: we've actually had a server together with the working prototype of a client app—all before writing even a single line of Kivy-related code.

As a general rule, it helps immensely to build your software in such an order so that you can test every part of it immediately. I'm not talking about **test-driven development** (TDD) here, as it's arguable whether full-fledged, exclusively test-driven programming helps the cause or not. But even just being able to fiddle with each piece of functionality as it comes together is infinitely more productive than writing a huge pile of code up front.

Finally, Kivy is well-equipped when it comes to networked GUI apps. For example, the Twisted integration that we used in the previous chapter, and the support for loading textures over the network—these things help immensely to build multi-user, Internet apps.

Now, let's jump to another topic altogether: Kivy game development.

6
Making the 2048 Game

In the next few chapters, we will build a series of increasingly complex game projects to demonstrate some of the concepts commonly associated with game development: state management, controls, sound effects, and fast shader-based graphics, to name a few.

An important thing to consider upfront is that no approach is actually unique to game development: there are whole other classes of software that use the same algorithms and performance hacks as video games.

However, let's start small and gradually work our way to complex things. Our first project is re-implementing the relatively well-known **2048** board game.

This chapter will shed light on a number of Kivy techniques that are practically required when developing games:

- Creating Kivy widgets with custom visual appearance and behavior
- Drawing on canvas and utilizing built-in graphics instructions
- Using absolute positioning to arrange widgets arbitrarily on screen (as opposed to relying on a structured layout)
- Moving widgets smoothly using Kivy's built-in support for animations

Positioning widgets in absolute coordinates may sound like a regression after getting used to layout classes, but it's necessary in highly interactive applications such as games. For example, a rectangular playing field of many board games can be represented by a `GridLayout`, but even a basic animation such as movement from cell to cell will be tricky to implement. Such a task is doomed to include widget reparenting in some form; this alone pretty much marginalizes any gains from using a fixed layout.

About the game

For the uninitiated, the game of 2048 is a math puzzle where you combine numbers to get to 2048 and possibly beyond that, to 4096 and 8192 (albeit this may prove challenging, so 2048 is a sufficiently hard-to-achieve winning condition). The board is a 4×4 square grid. It is mostly empty at first, with a few **2** tiles. Each turn the player moves all tiles in the same direction of choice: up, right, down, or left. If a tile cannot advance in that direction (there is no free space available), then it stays put in place.

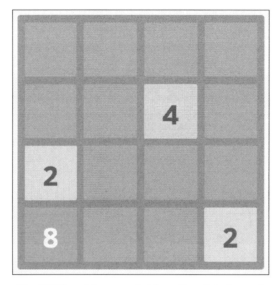

The 2048 board (a screenshot from the original game)

When two tiles having the same value touch (or rather, attempt to move on top of one another), they merge into one and sum up, increasing the tile nominal to a next power of two. So the progression looks like this: 2, 4, 8, 16, ... , 2048 and so on; programmers usually find this sequence familiar. After each turn, another **2** tile is spawned in a random empty space.

The original version of 2048 also sometimes creates **4** instead of **2**; this is a minor feature that won't be addressed in this chapter, but should be rather simple to implement.

The game ends if there are no valid moves available to the player (the board is filled up in an unfortunate combination where no tiles of the same value are next to each other). You can play the original game of 2048 at `http://gabrielecirulli.github.io/2048/`.

Gameplay concepts and overview

Games are generally very much stateful: the application goes through a number of distinctive states, such as the start screen, world map, town screen, and so on, depending on the specifics of the game. Certainly, each game is very different and there aren't many aspects that are common across a significant number of games.

One such aspect, and very basic at that, is that most games have either a win or a loss condition, often both. This may sound trivial, but these conditions and associated game states may have a tremendous impact on player's engagement and perception of the game.

There are games that are completely endless by design and have no connotation of the "game over" state (neither win nor loss) within the rules, and they are incredibly hard to get right in terms of player motivation. Such games also commonly provide a state of strong local advantage and disadvantage to compensate.

For example, while you cannot win the game or die completely and get into a "game over" state in World of Warcraft, or numerous other MMORPG titles that followed the same design concepts, you are certainly punished for neglecting your character's health and stats by having to perform in-game revival and associated tasks like repairing broken equipment.

Also, if you're exceptionally good, oftentimes you can team up with other highly skilled players and obtain items that aren't otherwise obtainable (and hence are unavailable to bad or casual players). This includes numerous boss encounters, raids, and those hard-to-get achievements.

The aforementioned losing condition found in 2048—the game ends when there are no available moves on the board—works great in practice because it makes the game gradually harder towards the end.

At the very beginning, the game isn't difficult at all: the player can basically perform completely random moves without any strategy. New tiles are added to the board having the same value, so it's impossible to fill all cells and run out of valid moves during first few turns, even on purpose—all the tiles are compatible and can be combined, no matter which direction the player chooses to move.

However, as you progress further in the game and variation is introduced to the board, free cells become increasingly scarcer. Since different values cannot be merged together, board management quickly becomes a problem.

Gameplay mechanics is what makes 2048 so engaging: it's really easy to start, the rules are simple and don't change over the course of the game, and 2048 doesn't punish experimentation in the beginning, even in the form of clearly suboptimal behavior, until much later in the game.

Randomness, or lack thereof

Since all tiles (up to 16) move at once, some of the resulting situations may have not been foreseen by players if they don't pay close attention. Albeit completely deterministic, this algorithm is perceived as having a touch of randomness to it. This also helps engagement by making 2048 feel more like an arcade game, slightly unpredictable and surprising.

This is generally a good thing: random encounters (or more accurately, encounters that are perceived as random, like in this case) may add life to an otherwise linear process, making the gameplay more interesting.

The 2048 project outline

To summarize, the following are the defining characteristics of the game:

* The playing field (the board) is 4×4 cells
* The following actions occur during each turn:
    ◦ Player moves all tiles in a direction of choice
    ◦ Colliding two tiles having the same value produces one tile of greater value
    ◦ New **2** tile is spawned in empty space
* The player wins by creating a **2048** tile
* The game ends when there are no valid moves left (that is, none of the possible moves can change the situation on the board anymore)

This checklist will come in handy later on, as it forms the essential technical outline of what we're going to implement in this chapter.

What makes 2048 a good choice of project?

One might ask whether re-implementing an existing game is a sound idea. The answer is, by all means, yes; a more detailed explanation follows.

This is slightly off-topic when talking about practical software development, but the rationale to recreate a well-known project may not be obvious. If this chapter's approach makes perfect sense to you without lengthy explanations, then feel free to skip to the next section where the actual development begins.

To support the choice of 2048 (and the approach of "re-implementing the wheel" as a whole), let's first assume the following: game development is extremely challenging on many different levels:

- Interesting game designs are hard to come by. There has to be a central idea to game mechanics, which may require a healthy amount of creativity.

- A good game requires that gameplay isn't way too complex, which may quickly lead to frustration, but not too easy and therefore boring either. Balancing this may sound simple at first, but is usually hard to get right.

- Some algorithms are harder than others. Path-finding on a flat, tiled map is easily approachable, but path-finding in a dynamic arbitrary three-dimensional space is a whole other story; **artificial intelligence** (**AI**) for a shooter may be simplistic and still deliver excellent results, while AI for a strategy game has to be clever and unpredictable to provide sufficient challenge and variety.

- The attention to detail and the amount of polish that makes a good game can be downright overwhelming, even to professionals working in the field.

This list is by no means exhaustive and serves not to scare everyone away from game development, but to get the point across—there are many things that can go wrong, so don't hesitate to offload some of the tasks to a third party. This increases your chances of delivering a working project and reduces the associated amount of frustration.

A go-to approach in gamedev (especially a sporadic, zero-budget effort like this book's projects) is to avoid costly creative search, especially in terms of gameplay. If you cannot get the project out of the door, its uniqueness is of very little value. That's why one should reuse as many existing elements as possible when building a new game.

You don't have to copy someone else's ideas verbatim, of course—tweaking every aspect of the game can be fun and a very rewarding endeavor.

In fact, most games borrow ideas, gameplay, and sometimes even visual attributes from their predecessors, and there is very little variety overall (this isn't necessarily a good thing, just the state of today's industry, for better or worse).

Simplicity as a feature

Getting back to the 2048 game, it's worth noting that its rules are very simple, borderline trivial. The fun factor, however, is inexplicably high; 2048 was very popular for a relatively long time, with numerous spin-offs flooding the Internet and app stores.

This alone makes the game of 2048 well worth rebuilding from scratch, even more so for the purpose of learning. Let's assume that at this point you're entirely convinced that 2048 is a fantastic choice of a project, and are eager to move on to actual development.

Creating the 2048 board

Up until now, we were relying on existing Kivy widgets, customizing them as needed to fit our specific use case. For this application, we're going to build our own unique widgets: Board (the playing field) and Tile.

Let's begin with the simple stuff and create the background for the playing field. The most unimaginative way to do so would be just using a static image; this approach has many problems, for example, it does not support the multitude of possible screen sizes properly (remember that we're talking about both desktop and mobile at the same time, so the screen size can vary wildly).

Instead, we will create the Board widget that renders the playing field graphics onto its canvas. This way, the board's positioning and size will be given declaratively in a Kivy language file, same as with other widgets we've used before (such as text labels and buttons).

Probably the easiest thing to start with is indeed setting the position and size of a board. To do this efficiently, we can use FloatLayout; this is one of the simplest layout classes provided by Kivy, which uses just the size and position hints. The following listing pretty much summarizes the usage of FloatLayout (this code resides in the game.kv file):

```
#:set padding 20

FloatLayout:
    Board:
        id: board
        pos_hint: {'center_x': 0.5, 'center_y': 0.5}
        size_hint: (None, None)
        center: root.center
        size: [min(root.width, root.height) - 2 * padding] * 2
```

Here, the `Board` widget is centered on the screen, both vertically and horizontally. In order to account for any possible screen orientation or aspect ratio, we compute board size by picking the smaller side of the screen (either width or height) and subtracting the padding twice (we want the same gap from both sides). The board is square, so its dimensions are equal.

The `[...] * 2` trick on the `size:` line is a fairly standard Python feature to avoid repeating the same value in a list or tuple many times over when initializing the data structure, for example, `[1] * 3` equals `[1, 1, 1]`.

To avoid confusion with the arithmetic multiplication, we employ this feature sparingly. However, in production you should consider using this syntax where appropriate, as it's more concise than writing the same repetitive list or tuple by hand.

In order to see the result of our work so far, we need to define the `Board` widget itself and make it render something (by default, empty widgets are completely invisible). This will take place in the `main.py` file:

```
from kivy.graphics import BorderImage
from kivy.uix.widget import Widget

spacing = 15

class Board(Widget):
    def __init__(self, **kwargs):
        super(Board, self).__init__(**kwargs)
        self.resize()

    def resize(self, *args):
        self.cell_size = (0.25 * (self.width - 5 * spacing), ) * 2
        self.canvas.before.clear()
        with self.canvas.before:
            BorderImage(pos=self.pos, size=self.size,
                        source='board.png')

    on_pos = resize
    on_size = resize
```

Similar to the definition of `padding` in `game.kv`, we define `spacing` at the top of the Python source code. This is the distance between two adjacent cells and from an edge of the board to an edge of the nearby cell.

The `resize()` method plays a central role in this part of the code: it's called when the `Board` widget is created (directly from `__init__()`) or repositioned (with the help of `on_pos` and `on_size` event callbacks). If the widget was indeed resized, we compute the new `cell_size` up front; it's a very simple computation actually, so it won't hurt even if the size of the widget did not change between invocations:

$$cell\ size = \frac{board\ size - (num.\ cells + 1) \times spacing}{number\ of\ cells}$$

Here, *size* means either width or height, since all objects in question are square.

Next, we render the background. We clear the `canvas.before` graphics instruction group and fill it with primitives (which are represented by just `BorderImage` at the moment). The `canvas.before` group, as opposed to `canvas.after` or just `canvas`, is executed first when a widget is being rendered. This makes it perfect for background imagery that needs to be below any child other graphics.

Canvas instruction groups are Kivy's way of organizing lower-level graphical operations, such as copying image data to canvas, drawing lines, and performing raw OpenGL calls. For a brief introduction to using the canvas, refer to *Chapter 2, Building a Paint App*.

Individual canvas instructions, living in the `kivy.graphics` namespace, are conceptually children of a `canvas` object (or `canvas.before` and `canvas.after`), just like leaf widgets are children of a container or root widget. Hierarchical definitions in code also look very similar.

An important difference, however, is that widgets have a complex lifecycle, can align themselves on the screen, respond to events, and do more. Rendering instructions, on the contrary, are just that—mostly self-contained primitives for drawing. For example, the `Color` instruction changes the color (tint) for next instructions in queue, if any; `Image` draws an image on canvas; and so on.

For now, the background is just a rectangle. It has rounded corners, thanks to the background image, `board.png`, rendered using the `BorderImage` instruction—a 9-patch technique described in *Chapter 1, Building a Clock App*, similar to how bordered buttons were implemented in all previous examples over the course of this book.

Going through cells

Our playing field is two-dimensional, and traversing a two-dimensional array can be achieved in a very obvious fashion by nesting `for` loops like this:

```
for x in range(4):
    for y in range(4):
        # code that uses cell at (x, y)
```

Not only is this unwieldy and adds two levels of indentation, but also leads to repetitive code when used in many places throughout the program, which is undesirable. In Python, we can refactor this code using a generator function as shown here:

```
# In main.py
def all_cells():
    for x in range(4):
        for y in range(4):
            yield (x, y)
```

The generator function itself looks similar to the straightforward approach shown in the previous code snippet. Its usage, however, is clearer:

```
for x, y in all_cells():
    # code that uses cell at (x, y)
```

This is basically the same code running two nested loops, but the details of those are abstracted, and as such we have a tidy one-liner, which is also more customizable than the code interspersed with literal `for` loops over each coordinate.

In the following code, we will refer to board coordinates (those that designate a board cell, as opposed to pixel coordinates of rendered objects on screen) as `board_x` and `board_y`.

Rendering empty cells

The position and size of the game board as a whole are defined by placement of the `Board` widget, but the location of individual cells is yet undefined. Next, we're going to compute each cell's coordinates on screen and draw all cells on the canvas.

The location of a cell on screen, taking `spacing` into account, can be calculated as follows:

```
# In main.py
class Board(Widget):
    def cell_pos(self, board_x, board_y):
        return (self.x + board_x *
```

```
            (self.cell_size[0] + spacing) + spacing,
    self.y + board_y *
            (self.cell_size[1] + spacing) + spacing)
```

Canvas operations typically expect absolute coordinates, and this is why we're adding the `Board` location (`self.x`, `self.y`) to the computed value.

Now that we can iterate over the playing field and compute an onscreen position of each cell based on its board location, the only thing that's left is actually rendering cells on the canvas. Tweaking the `canvas.before` code as follows should suffice:

```
from kivy.graphics import Color, BorderImage
from kivy.utils import import get_color_from_hex

with self.canvas.before:
    BorderImage(pos=self.pos, size=self.size,
                source='board.png')
    Color(*get_color_from_hex('CCC0B4'))
    for board_x, board_y in all_cells():
        BorderImage(pos=self.cell_pos(board_x, board_y),
                    size=self.cell_size,
                    source='cell.png')
```

When rendering images, the `Color` instruction serves the same purpose as we've discussed previously in this book (for example, in *Chapter 2, Building a Paint App*): it allows every tile to be colored differently while using the same (white) image for a texture.

Also, note the use of `cell_pos` and `cell_size` — these are the *real* screen coordinates in pixels. They vary according to the application's window size, and are generally computed just to draw something on the screen. For game logic, we are going to use much simpler board coordinates `board_x` and `board_y`.

This screenshot summarizes all work we've done so far:

The playing field, devoid of anything remotely interesting yet

Board data structure

To be able to work on game logic, we need to keep an internal representation of the board. For this, we will use a simple two-dimensional array (to be technically correct, a list of lists). The blank state of the board looks like this:

```
[[None, None, None, None],
 [None, None, None, None],
 [None, None, None, None],
 [None, None, None, None]]
```

The value of None means the cell is empty. The described data structure can be initialized using the nested list comprehension, as shown in the following code fragment:

```
class Board(Widget):
    b = None

    def reset(self):
        self.b = [[None for i in range(4)]
                  for j in range(4)]
```

We call the preceding function reset() because, in addition to initializing the data structure beforehand, it will also be used to return the game to a blank state after a game-over situation.

The use of list comprehensions isn't strictly necessary; this notation is just more concise than the literal list of lists which is also shown earlier. If you think that the literal form (as shown earlier) is more readable, by all means use it instead when initializing the grid.

Variable naming

A short name, b, is deemed appropriate because this property should be considered internal to the class, so it doesn't take part in the external API (or lack thereof). We will also use this variable heavily in the following code, so this also serves to reduce typing, akin to the commonly used loop iterator variables i and j.

In Python, private fields are usually designated with the leading underscore, for example, _name. We do not follow this convention strictly here, partly because this looks bad when used with very short names. This whole class is largely internal to the application anyway and barely, if at all, reusable as a separate module.

Consider Board.b a local variable for all intents and purposes, especially since Board acts as a singleton in our app: there should be only one instance of it at a given time.

Calling reset()

We should call `Board.reset()` at the beginning of the game to initialize the internal representation of the board. The right place to do so is the application's `on_start` callback, as shown in the following code snippet:

```
# In main.py
from kivy.app import App

class GameApp(App):
    def on_start(self):
        board = self.root.ids.board
        board.reset()
```

Testing passability

We don't have anything clever to put in the grid yet, but this doesn't prevent us from writing a passability check, `can_move()`. This helper function tests whether we can place a tile at the specified location on the board.

The check is two-fold. First we need to make sure that the coordinates that are provided generally make sense (that is, don't fall outside the board), and this check will live in a separate function called `valid_cell()`. Then, we look up the board cell to see if it's empty (equals to `None`). The return value will be `True` if the move is legal and the cell is free, and `False` otherwise.

The preceding sentence can be literally translated to Python:

```
# In main.py, under class Board:
def valid_cell(self, board_x, board_y):
    return (board_x >= 0 and board_y >= 0 and
            board_x <= 3 and board_y <= 3)

def can_move(self, board_x, board_y):
    return (self.valid_cell(board_x, board_y) and
            self.b[board_x][board_y] is None)
```

These methods will be used later when writing the code responsible for tile movement. But first, we need to create the tiles.

Making tiles

This part of the chapter is devoted to building the `Tile` widget. Tiles are more dynamic in nature than, for example, the `Board` widget that we've seen earlier. To account for this, we are going to create a number of Kivy properties on the `Tile` class so that any visible change to tile automatically leads to redrawing it.

Kivy properties differ from regular Python ones: a property in Python is basically just a variable bound to an instance of class, possibly coupled with getter and setter functions. In Kivy, properties have an additional feature: they emit events when changed and as such you can observe interesting properties and adjust other related variables accordingly, or perhaps repaint the screen.

Most of this work happens under the hood without your intervention: when you issue a change to, for example, the `pos` or `size` of a widget, an event (`on_pos` or `on_size` respectively) is fired.

Interestingly, all properties that are defined in a `.kv` file are propagated automatically. For example, you can write things such as:

```
Label:
    pos: root.pos
```

When the `root.pos` property changes, so does this label's `pos` value; they are kept in sync effortlessly.

We are going to use this quality to our advantage when creating the `Tile` widget. First, let's declare interesting properties that should be accounted for when rendering the widget:

```
# In main.py
from kivy.properties import ListProperty, NumericProperty

class Tile(Widget):
    font_size = NumericProperty(24)
    number = NumericProperty(2)  # Text shown on the tile
    color = ListProperty(get_color_from_hex(tile_colors[2]))
    number_color = ListProperty(get_color_from_hex('776E65'))
```

This is all that's needed to draw a tile; property names should be rather self-explanatory, with the possible exception of `color`, a tile's background color. The `number` property denotes the *face value* of the tile.

If you want to run this code right now, please replace `tile_colors[2]` with a literal color value, for example, `'#EEE4DA'`. We will define the `tile_colors` list properly later in this section.

Next, in `game.kv`, we define graphical elements that constitute our widget:

```
<Tile>:
    canvas:
        Color:
            rgb: self.color

        BorderImage:
            pos: self.pos
            size: self.size
            source: 'cell.png'

    Label:
        pos: root.pos
        size: root.size
        bold: True
        color: root.number_color
        font_size: root.font_size
        text: str(root.number)
```

Custom properties coming from the `Tile` class are highlighted. Note that inside the `canvas` declaration, `self` refers to `<Tile>`, and not to the canvas itself. This is because `canvas` is merely a property of the corresponding widget. `Label`, on the other hand, is a nested widget in its own right, so it uses `root.XXX` to refer to `<Tile>` properties. It's the top-level definition in this case, so it works.

Tile initialization

In the original 2048 game, tiles have varying background colors according to their numeric value. We are going to implement the same effect, and for this we need a color mapping, *number → color*.

The following list of colors is close to what the original 2048 game uses:

```
# In main.py
colors = (
    'EEE4DA', 'EDE0C8', 'F2B179', 'F59563',
    'F67C5F', 'F65E3B', 'EDCF72', 'EDCC61',
    'EDC850', 'EDC53F', 'EDC22E')
```

In order to map them to numbers, which in 2048 are powers of two, we can use the following code:

```
tile_colors = {2 ** i: color for i, color in
               enumerate(colors, start=1)}
```

This is exactly the mapping we need, with tile numbers as keys and corresponding colors as values:

```
{2: 'EEE4DA',
 4: 'EDE0C8',
 # ...
 1024: 'EDC53F',
 2048: 'EDC22E'}
```

With the colors in place, we can write an initializer of the `Tile` class, the `Tile.__init__` method. It will mostly just assign properties of the tile in question, as shown in the following listing:

```
class Tile(Widget):
    font_size = NumericProperty(24)
    number = NumericProperty(2)
    color = ListProperty(get_color_from_hex(tile_colors[2]))
    number_color = ListProperty(get_color_from_hex('776E65'))

    def __init__(self, number=2, **kwargs):
        super(Tile, self).__init__(**kwargs)
        self.font_size = 0.5 * self.width
        self.number = number
        self.update_colors()

    def update_colors(self):
        self.color = get_color_from_hex(
            tile_colors[self.number])
        if self.number > 4:
            self.number_color = \
                get_color_from_hex('F9F6F2')
```

Let's briefly talk about every property that we see here:

- `font_size`: This is set to half of `cell_size`. This is basically an arbitrary value which looks fine. We cannot just put an absolute font size here, because the board is scaled to fit the window; the best approach is to keep font size to scale.

- `number`: This is passed from the calling function and defaults to 2.

- color (the background color of a tile): This originates from the mapping discussed earlier, based on the value of number.

- number_color: This is chosen based on the number property, too, but with much less variety. There are just two colors: a dark one (the default) which is used on a light background, and a lighter one for better contrast on a bright background, as numbers go up; hence the check (if self.number > 4).

Everything else is passed to the superclass in the form of kwargs (keyword arguments). This includes position and size attributes, which coincidentally are the topic of the next section.

Colors live in a helper function of their own, update_colors(), because later we will need to update them when merging tiles.

It's worth mentioning that at this point, you can create a tile using something along the lines of:

```
tile = Tile(pos=self.cell_pos(x, y), size=self.cell_size)
self.add_widget(tile)
```

As a result, a new tile will be visible on the screen. (The preceding code should reside in the Board class. Alternatively, change all self references to an instance of Board.)

Resizing tiles

Another problem with tiles is that they aren't aware that they should keep up with the board being resized. If you enlarge or shrink the application window, the board adjusts its size and position, but tiles don't. We're going to fix that.

Let's start with a helper method for updating all relevant Tile properties at once:

```
class Tile(Widget):
    # Other methods skipped to save space

    def resize(self, pos, size):
        self.pos = pos
        self.size = size
        self.font_size = 0.5 * self.width
```

Although this method isn't strictly required, it makes the following code a bit more concise.

The actual resizing code will be located at the end of the `Board.resize()` method, which is invoked by Kivy property bindings. Here, we can iterate over all tiles and fix their metrics according to new values of `cell_size` and `cell_pos`:

```
def resize(self, *args):
    # Previously-seen code omitted

    for board_x, board_y in all_cells():
        tile = self.b[board_x][board_y]
        if tile:
            tile.resize(pos=self.cell_pos(board_x, board_y),
                        size=self.cell_size)
```

This approach is the exact opposite of automatic property binding we've seen earlier: we do all resizing in a centralized, explicit fashion. Some programmers may find this way of doing things more readable and less *magical* (for example, Python code allows you to set breakpoints inside event handlers and such; on the contrary, Kivy language files are much harder to meaningfully debug, should the need arise).

Implementing the game logic

Now that we've built all the components required to make an implementation of the 2048 game, let's move on to more interesting things: spawning, moving, and combining tiles.

It's only logical that we begin with spawning new tiles in random empty cells. The algorithm for doing so is as follows:

1. Find all cells that are currently empty.

2. Pick a random one from those found in step 1.

3. Create a new tile at the position determined in step 2.

4. Add it to the internal grid (`Board.b`), and to the board widget itself (using `add_widget()`) for Kivy to render it.

The sequence of actions should be self-evident; the following Python implementation of this algorithm is also very straightforward:

```
# In main.py, a method of class Board:
def new_tile(self, *args):
    empty_cells = [(x, y) for x, y in all_cells()  # Step 1
                   if self.b[x][y] is None]

    x, y = random.choice(empty_cells)  # Step 2
    tile = Tile(pos=self.cell_pos(x, y),  # Step 3
```

```
                       size=self.cell_size)
        self.b[x][y] = tile  # Step 4
        self.add_widget(tile)
```

New tiles spawn at the beginning of the game and after every move. We will get to moving tiles shortly, and we can already implement spawning tiles at the beginning:

```
def reset(self):
    self.b = [[None for i in range(4)]
              for j in range(4)]  # same as before
    self.new_tile()
    self.new_tile()  # put down 2 tiles
```

If you run the program after this change, you should see two tiles added to the board in random places.

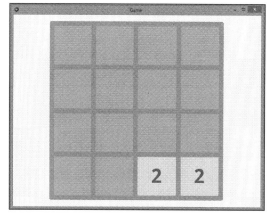

Spawning tiles in action

Moving tiles

To implement movement efficiently, we'll need to map every input event to a directional vector. Then, the `Board.move()` method will accept such a vector and rearrange the board accordingly. A directional vector is typically normalized (its length equals to one), and in our case, we can just add it to the current tile's coordinates to get its possible new location.

The 2048 game only allows four options for movement, so the keyboard mapping definition is very short:

```
from kivy.core.window import Keyboard

key_vectors = {
    Keyboard.keycodes['up']: (0, 1),
```

```
        Keyboard.keycodes['right']: (1, 0),
        Keyboard.keycodes['down']: (0, -1),
        Keyboard.keycodes['left']: (-1, 0),
    }
```

In this listing, we're referring to arrow keys, aptly named `'up'`, `'right'`, `'down'`, and `'left'` in Kivy's predefined `keycodes` dictionary.

Listening to keyboard events in Kivy can be implemented using the `Window.bind()` method, as shown in the following code:

```
# In main.py, under class Board:
def on_key_down(self, window, key, *args):
    if key in key_vectors:
        self.move(*key_vectors[key])

# Then, during the initialization (in GameApp.on_start())
Window.bind(on_key_down=board.on_key_down)
```

The `Board.move()` method gets called as a result. It accepts the directional vector components, `dir_x` and `dir_y`, unpacked from `key_vectors[key]`.

Controlling the iteration sequence

Before we get to actually build the `Board.move()` method, we need to make the `all_cells()` generator function customizable; correct iteration order depends on the movement direction.

For example, when going up, we have to start with the topmost cell in each column. This way we can ensure that all tiles will be arranged densely at the top of the board. In the event of incorrect iteration, you will inevitably see holes remaining from cells at the bottom bumping into cells at the top before those have reached their topmost available position.

Taking this new requirement into account, we can easily write a new version of the generator function as shown here:

```
def all_cells(flip_x=False, flip_y=False):
    for x in (reversed(range(4)) if flip_x else range(4)):
        for y in (reversed(range(4)) if flip_y else range(4)):
            yield (x, y)
```

You may also want to write just `(3, 2, 1, 0)` instead of `reversed(range(4))`. In this specific case, literal enumeration is more concise than the iterator that produces it. Whether you choose to do so is a matter of personal preference and doesn't affect the functionality in any way.

Implementing the move() method

Now, we can build the simplest version of the `Board.move()` function. At the moment, it will only facilitate moving tiles around, but we will soon upgrade it to also merge tiles together.

Here's an overview of this function's algorithm so far:

1. Go through all (existing) tiles.
2. For each tile, move it in the specified direction until it bumps into another tile or the playing field boundary.
3. If the tile's coordinates stay the same, continue to the next tile.
4. Animate the tile's transition to new coordinates and continue to the next tile.

The Python implementation closely follows the previous description:

```python
def move(self, dir_x, dir_y):
    for board_x, board_y in all_cells(dir_x > 0, dir_y > 0):
        tile = self.b[board_x][board_y]
        if not tile:
            continue

        x, y = board_x, board_y
        while self.can_move(x + dir_x, y + dir_y):
            self.b[x][y] = None
            x += dir_x
            y += dir_y
            self.b[x][y] = tile

        if x == board_x and y == board_y:
            continue  # nothing has happened

        anim = Animation(pos=self.cell_pos(x, y),
                         duration=0.25, transition='linear')
        anim.start(tile)
```

In this listing, you can see the usage of `can_move()` function that we've built earlier.

The `Animation` API works akin to CSS transitions in a browser. We need to provide:

- Values of properties we want to animate (in this example, `pos`)
- Duration, in seconds
- Transition type (`'linear'` means equal speed throughout the route)

Given all that, Kivy renders a smooth animation with the widget morphing from the current state to a new one.

 All transition types are detailed in the Kivy manual (http://kivy.org/docs/api-kivy.animation.html). There are just too many of them to provide a meaningful summary here.

Binding touch controls

Let's also implement touch controls (swipes) in addition to keyboard bindings that we've done previously. Thanks to mouse input events being processed just like touches in Kivy, our code will also support mouse gestures.

To do so, we need to merely add an event handler to the Board class:

```
from kivy.vector import Vector

# A method of class Board:
def on_touch_up(self, touch):
    v = Vector(touch.pos) - Vector(touch.opos)
    if v.length() < 20:
        return

    if abs(v.x) > abs(v.y):
        v.y = 0
    else:
        v.x = 0

    self.move(*v.normalize())
```

In this code, we're converting an arbitrary gesture to a unit vector that we need for Board.move() to work. The complete walkthrough is as follows:

1. The if v.length() < 20: condition checks for eliminating very short gestures. If the travel distance is very short, then probably it was a click or tap, not a swipe.

2. The if abs(v.x) > abs(v.y): condition sets the shorter component of the vector to zero. The remaining component thus designates the direction.

3. And then we simply normalize the vector and feed it into Board.move().

This last point is exactly the reason why you shouldn't invent your own ways to represent *mathematically expressible* things such as directions.

Everyone out there understands vectors, you get compatibility with any other library essentially for free when you use them; but should you reinvent the wheel and define some other representation, for example, UP = 0, RIGHT = 1 and so on—and boom, you're now all alone in the cold, dark nowhere, inconsistent with the rest of the world. Seriously, don't do that unless you have at least two very good reasons.

Combining tiles

We will discuss the last fun part of the gameplay now: merging tiles as they bump into one another. The following code is surprisingly not very convoluted; one would probably expect it to be harder than that.

We will build yet another helper function, can_combine(). Conceptually very similar to can_move(), this function returns True if we can combine the current tile with the one at the provided location, that is, if the coordinates are same and the location contains a tile having the same value.

This is the unabridged listing of the described method. Compare this function to its counterpart, can_move(), and you will notice that it looks almost identical:

```
def can_combine(self, board_x, board_y, number):
    return (self.valid_cell(board_x, board_y) and
            self.b[board_x][board_y] is not None and
            self.b[board_x][board_y].number == number)
```

With this function in place, we can now expand the Board.move() function to support merging cells.

Just add the following snippet after the movement while self.can_move() block:

```
if self.can_combine(x + dir_x, y + dir_y,
                    tile.number):
    self.b[x][y] = None
    x += dir_x
    y += dir_y
    self.remove_widget(self.b[x][y])
    self.b[x][y] = tile
    tile.number *= 2
    tile.update_colors()
```

> Please see the full source code for this project if you're unsure about the code layout. The latest version of all the source code accompanying this book can be found at https://github.com/mvasilkov/kb.

Again, this code resembles the movement logic, with two notable differences. The tile we're combining with gets removed using `remove_widget()`, and the remaining tile's number is updated, which means that we need to also update its colors.

So, our tiles merge happily and their values add up. The game would absolutely be playable at this point, if not for the last few things discussed next.

Adding more tiles

Our game really should spawn new tiles after each turn. To complicate things further, this has to be done at the end of the animation sequence, when tiles that were affected by the last turn are done moving.

Thankfully, there is a fitting event, `Animation.on_complete`, which is exactly what we're going to use here. Since we run a number of animations equal to the number of active tiles simultaneously, we need to bind the event only to the first `Animation` instance—they all start at the same time and have the same duration anyway, so there shouldn't be a noticeable difference between the timings of the first and the last animation in a synchronized batch.

The implementation resides in the same `Board.move()` method that we've seen previously:

```
def move(self, dir_x, dir_y):
    moving = False

    # Large portion of the code is omitted to save trees

        if x == board_x and y == board_y:
            continue  # nothing has happened

        anim = Animation(pos=self.cell_pos(x, y),
                         duration=0.25, transition='linear')
        if not moving:
            anim.on_complete = self.new_tile
            moving = True

        anim.start(tile)
```

As soon as the animation ends and the `on_complete` event fires, `new_tile()` is called and the game continues.

The reason we introduce a Boolean flag named `moving` is to ensure that `new_tile()` won't be called more than once per turn. Skipping this check leads to the board getting flooded with new titles in no time.

Synchronizing turns

You might have noticed that there is a bug in the current implementation of animated tiles: the player can start a new turn before the previous one has ended. The easiest way to reproduce and obviate this issue is to increase the duration of the movement considerably, for example, to 10 seconds:

```
# This is for demonstration only
anim = Animation(pos=self.cell_pos(x, y),
                 duration=10, transition='linear')
```

The easiest way we can fix this bug is by ignoring subsequent calls to `move()` while the tiles are in motion already. In order to do that, we have to broaden the scope of the previously seen `moving` flag. From now on, it will be a property of the `Board` class. We are also adjusting the `move()` method accordingly:

```
class Board(Widget):
    moving = False

    def move(self, dir_x, dir_y):
        if self.moving:
            return

        # Again, large portion of the code is omitted

        anim = Animation(pos=self.cell_pos(x, y),
                         duration=0.25,
                         transition='linear')
        if not self.moving:
            anim.on_complete = self.new_tile
            self.moving = True

        anim.start(tile)
```

Don't forget to reset `moving` back to `False` in `new_tile()`, or else tiles will cease to move at all after the first turn.

Game over

One more thing that is missing from the game is the "game over" state. We discussed winning and losing conditions at the beginning of the chapter, so it's stylistically appropriate to end the implementation with the same topic.

The winning condition

Testing whether the player has managed to assemble a 2048 tile can be easily done in the only place where the tile value is doubled when combining tiles in the `Board.move()` function:

```
tile.number *= 2
if (tile.number == 2048):
    print('You win the game')
```

Note that the specific UI for reporting end game conditions is purposefully omitted. Creating yet another simple screen with a button and some text would unnecessarily clutter the chapter without adding anything to the content already present in the book.

In other words, implementing visually appealing end game states is again left as an exercise—we will only suggest an algorithm for detecting them.

To test end game conditions, it may be useful to lower the winning requirement severely by replacing 2048 by, for example, 64, but don't forget to change it back before a public release!

The loss condition

This algorithm is a bit more complex, and as such it can be written in a number of ways. Probably the most literal approach would be to traverse the board completely before each move to test whether the board is deadlocked:

```
def is_deadlocked(self):
    for x, y in all_cells():
        if self.b[x][y] is None:
            return False  # Step 1

        number = self.b[x][y].number
        if self.can_combine(x + 1, y, number) or \
                self.can_combine(x, y + 1, number):
            return False  # Step 2
    return True  # Step 3
```

The explanation: for every tile on the board we're testing the following:

1. Found an empty cell? This instantly means that we're not deadlocked—another tile can move to that cell.

2. Otherwise, if the selected tile can combine with the one to the right or to the bottom, we're good, since we have a possible move.

3. If all else fails and we cannot find a cell that satisfies either of the previous conditions, this means we're out of moves—the game is over at this point.

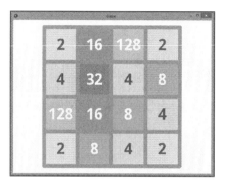

Game over: there are no valid moves

A fitting place to run this test would be in the `new_tile()` method:

```
def new_tile(self, *args):
    empty_cells = [(x, y) for x, y in all_cells()
                   if self.b[x][y] is None]

    # Spawning a new tile (omitted)

    if len(empty_cells) == 1 and self.is_deadlocked():
        print('Game over (board is deadlocked)')

    self.moving = False  # See above, "Synchronizing turns"
```

The precondition (`len(empty_cells) == 1`) allows us to run the check less often: there is no point in testing for the loss when the board isn't full yet. It's worth noting that our `is_deadlocked()` method would have correctly returned `False` in this case anyway, so this is purely an optimization, not affecting the "business logic" in any way.

This approach is still a little suboptimal, performance-wise, and could be improved at the cost of lengthening the code: one obvious optimization would be skipping the last row and column, and then not checking for bounds on each iteration, which `can_combine()` function implicitly does.

However, the gain in this case would be negligible, since this check runs at most once every turn, and we're mostly waiting for user input anyway.

Where to go from here

The game is finally playable, but there certainly are many areas in which it can be improved. If you're willing to toy with the concept of 2048 some more, consider some of the following tasks:

- Add more animations—they do wonders in terms of perceived interactivity.

- As an additional motivational factor, add a score counter and the related infrastructure (for instance, the ability to save high scores and transmit them to the global server-side leaderboard).

- Tweak the game rules so that they are exactly like the original 2048 game.

- For a more mind-bending experimentation, build an algorithm that predicts fruitless game sessions in advance. As a player, I would positively love to receive a notification that reads, "No matter what you do, in 7 turns it's over for you, thanks for playing."

- Change the rules completely. Add a multiplayer arena death match mode—be creative.

 If you're interested in seeing another, more complete Kivy implementation of the same 2048 game, take a look at `https://github.com/tito/2048`. This project, written by a core Kivy developer Mathieu Virbel, features Google Play integration, achievements, and a high-score leaderboard, among other things.

It should be postulated that reading other people's code is a great way to learn.

Summary

In this chapter, we built a playable replica of the 2048 game. We also showcased a number of implementation details that can be reused in other similar projects:

- Creating a scalable board that fits the screen in any resolution and orientation

- Putting together custom tiles, and implementing smooth movement for those with the help of Kivy's `Animation` API

- Mapping player's controls to both touch screen gestures and keyboard arrow keys at the same time, to account for any control scheme the user might expect from the game

The Kivy framework supports game development nicely; in particular, canvas rendering and support for animations can be very useful when building video games. Prototyping in Kivy is also feasible, albeit somewhat harder to do than in JavaScript (a modern browser is a very powerful platform, and it's especially hard to beat when it comes to cheap prototyping).

The resulting Python program is also inherently cross-platform unless you're using an OS-specific API in a way that prevents other systems from functioning. This means that technically your game can be played by everyone, reaching the widest possible audience.

The use of Kivy also doesn't conflict with publishing your work on major app distribution platforms, be it Apple AppStore, Google Play, or even Steam.

Certainly, Kivy lacks a great many features and most of the toolchain if compared to a full-fledged game engine like the Unreal Engine or Unity. This is due to the fact that Kivy is a general purpose UI framework and not a game engine per se; one can argue that such a comparison of vastly different software categories over respective feature sets is incorrect.

To summarize, Kivy is a solid choice for sporadic indie game development. Angry Birds could have been implemented in Python and Kivy by *you*! Imagine the scale of the opportunity you've missed back then. (But please don't feel bad about this, it was meant as an encouragement. Rovio's path to a successful game title wasn't exactly easy either.)

This brings us to the topic of the next chapter: writing an arcade game using Kivy. It will utilize the familiar concept of Kivy widgets in a variety of unorthodox ways to create an interactive side-scrolling environment, reminiscent of another critically acclaimed indie game, Flappy Bird.

7
Writing a Flappy Bird Clone

In *Chapter 6*, *Making the 2048 Game*, we already fiddled with simple game development, exemplified by the well-known **2048** puzzle. This is the logical continuation: we're going to build an arcade game, more specifically a **Flappy Bird**-style side scroller.

Flappy Bird is an incredibly simple yet very addictive mobile game released by Dong Nguyen back in 2013; by the end of January 2014, it was the most downloaded free game in the iOS App Store. The Flappy Bird phenomenon is very interesting, game design-wise. The game features exactly one action (tap anywhere on screen to bump the bird, changing its trajectory) and one player activity (fly through gaps in obstacles without touching them). This simple and repetitive gameplay has become quite a trend lately, as explained in the following section.

Asceticism in mobile game design

The *classical* two-dimensional arcade genre was recently reborn on mobile. There are currently lots of commercial re-issues of retro games, with the price tag being about the only difference from the original 30-year-old titles—these include Dizzy, Sonic, Double Dragon, and R-Type, to name a few.

One huge letdown many of these games share in a new environment is control scheme awkwardness: the touch screen and gyroscope that are commonly present in modern gadgets just don't replace a gamepad very well, if at all. This fact also became a selling point of new titles—designing a game from the ground up with the available control scheme in mind can be a huge win.

Some developers tackled with this problem by radically simplifying things upfront: it turns out that there is a huge market for simplistic toys, especially for low-cost or free (optionally, ad-supported) titles.

Games that feature very limited controls and gameplay can indeed become very popular, and Flappy Bird just landed in a sweet spot, providing extremely challenging yet minimalistic and easily accessible gameplay. In this chapter, we will be re-implementing this particular gem of a game design using Kivy. We are going to introduce a number of new things:

- Simulating very simple arcade physics
- Using Kivy widgets as fully featured game sprites, complete with arbitrary positioning and two-dimensional transformations, such as rotation
- Implementing basic collision detection
- Producing and implementing sound effects for games

The game we're building doesn't have a winning condition, and the slightest collision with an obstacle ends the game. In the original Flappy Bird title, players competed for a higher score (number of pipes passed without crashing into something). Similar to the previous chapter though, the implementation of a scoreboard is purposefully left out as an exercise for you.

Project overview

We're aiming to create a game conceptually similar to the original Flappy Bird, but with different visuals. It's unimaginatively called **Kivy Bird**. The end result is depicted as follows:

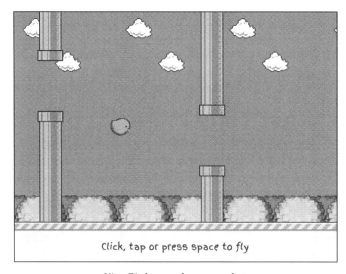

Kivy Bird gameplay screenshot

Let's take a closer look at the game and dissect it into logical parts, creating a project outline that will be used for development:

- **Background**: The scenery consists of a number of layers moving at different speeds, resulting in a neat fake depth (parallax effect). The movement is constant and not related to any game events; this makes the background an ideal starting point for the implementation.

- **Obstacles (pipes)**: This is a separate graphical layer that also advances towards the player at a constant speed. As opposed to the background, the pipes are procedurally adjusted to have different relative heights, keeping the gap between them passable for the player. A collision with a pipe ends the game.

- **Playable character (the bird)**: This sprite moves only vertically, constantly falling down. The player bumps it by clicking or tapping anywhere on the screen, this pushes the bird upwards. As soon as the bird meets floor, ceiling, or a pipe, the game ends.

This is roughly the order in which we're going to write the implementation.

Creating an animated background

We are going to use the following images to create the background for our game:

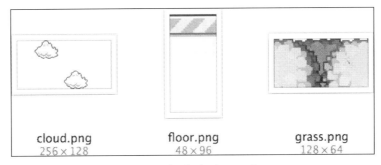

Images for the background

Note that all of these can be seamlessly tiled horizontally—this isn't a strict requirement, but a desirable property nonetheless, as the background looks nicer this way.

As mentioned in the description, the background is always in motion, disconnected from the rest of the game. This effect can be achieved in at least two ways:

- Using the straightforward approach, we can just move a huge textured polygon (or any number of polygons) in the background. Creating seamless looping animation in this case may require a bit of work.

- A more efficient way to achieve the same visual effect is to create a number of static polygons (one per layer) that span the whole viewport, and then animate just texture coordinates. With a tileable texture, this approach produces seamless and visually pleasing results, and amounts to less work overall—there is no need to reposition objects.

We will implement the second approach, as it's both easier and more effective. Let's start with the `kivybird.kv` file that contains the layout:

```
FloatLayout:
    Background:
        id: background
        canvas:
            Rectangle:
                pos: self.pos
                size: (self.width, 96)
                texture: self.tx_floor

            Rectangle:
                pos: (self.x, self.y + 96)
                size: (self.width, 64)
                texture: self.tx_grass

            Rectangle:
                pos: (self.x, self.height - 144)
                size: (self.width, 128)
                texture: self.tx_cloud
```

 All "magic numbers" from here on refer mostly to texture dimensions: 96 is the ground level, 64 is the height of grass, and 144 is a somewhat arbitrary level of clouds. Hardcoding things like that in production code is usually frowned upon, but we shall do it occasionally for the sake of simplicity and to minimize code size of examples.

As you can see, there are no moving parts here at all, just three rectangles positioned along the top and bottom edges of the screen. This scene depends on textures being exposed as properties (beginning with tx_) of the Background class, which we're going to implement next.

Loading tileable textures

We shall start with the helper function for loading tileable textures: this functionality will be used a lot in the following code, so it's a good idea to abstract it up front.

One way to do so is creating an intermediate Widget subclass, which will then serve as a base class for our custom widgets (in main.py):

```
from kivy.core.image import Image
from kivy.uix.widget import Widget

class BaseWidget(Widget):
    def load_tileable(self, name):
        t = Image('%s.png' % name).texture
        t.wrap = 'repeat'
        setattr(self, 'tx_%s' % name, t)
```

The bit that warrants creating the helper function is t.wrap = 'repeat'. We need to apply this to every tiled texture.

While we're at that, we also store the newly loaded texture using the naming convention of tx_ followed by the filename of an image. For example, a call to load_tileable('grass') will load the file called grass.png and store the resulting texture in a self.tx_grass attribute. This naming logic should be easy to follow.

The Background widget

Being able to conveniently load textures, we can now implement the Background widget as follows:

```
from kivy.properties import ObjectProperty

class Background(BaseWidget):
    tx_floor = ObjectProperty(None)
    tx_grass = ObjectProperty(None)
    tx_cloud = ObjectProperty(None)

    def __init__(self, **kwargs):
        super(Background, self).__init__(**kwargs)
```

```
for name in ('floor', 'grass', 'cloud'):
    self.load_tileable(name)
```

If you run the code at this point, you'll see distorted textures stretched to fill corresponding rectangles; this happens in the absence of explicitly given texture coordinates. To fix this, we need to adjust the `uvsize` property of each texture, which denotes how many times a texture is repeated to fill a polygon. For example, a `uvsize` of `(2, 2)` means that a texture fills one fourth of a rectangle.

This helper method will be used to set `uvsize` to an appropriate value so that our textures aren't distorted:

```
def set_background_size(self, tx):
    tx.uvsize = (self.width / tx.width, -1)
```

 Negative texture coordinates, as seen in this example, mean that the texture gets flipped. Kivy uses this effect to avoid costly raster operations, shifting the load to the GPU (graphics card), which is designed to handle these operations with ease.

This method depends on the width of a background, so it's appropriate to invoke it every time the widget's `size` property changes, using the `on_size()` callback. This keeps each texture's `uvsize` in sync, for example, when the user resizes the application window manually:

```
def on_size(self, *args):
    for tx in (self.tx_floor, self.tx_grass, self.tx_cloud):
        self.set_background_size(tx)
```

If done properly, the code so far produces a background similar to the following:

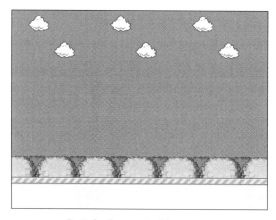

Static background with textures

Animating the background

The last thing that we need to do before moving on to other parts of the application is a background animation. First, we add a monotonous timer running at roughly 60 ticks per second to the `KivyBirdApp` application class:

```
from kivy.app import App
from kivy.clock import Clock

class KivyBirdApp(App):
    def on_start(self):
        self.background = self.root.ids.background
        Clock.schedule_interval(self.update, 0.016)

    def update(self, nap):
        self.background.update(nap)
```

The `update()` method just passes control to a similar method of the `Background` widget for now. The scope of this method is going to expand later, when we have more moving parts in our program.

In `Background.update()`, we change the texture origin (namely, a property called `uvpos`) to simulate movement:

```
def update(self, nap):
    self.set_background_uv('tx_floor', 2 * nap)
    self.set_background_uv('tx_grass', 0.5 * nap)
    self.set_background_uv('tx_cloud', 0.1 * nap)

def set_background_uv(self, name, val):
    t = getattr(self, name)
    t.uvpos = ((t.uvpos[0] + val) % self.width, t.uvpos[1])
    self.property(name).dispatch(self)
```

Again, the interesting stuff happens in a helper function, `set_background_uv()`:

- It increments the first component of the `uvpos` property, shifting the texture origin horizontally

- It calls `dispatch()` on the texture property, signaling that it has changed

Canvas instructions (in `kivybird.kv`) listen to this change and react accordingly, rendering the texture with updated origin. This results in a smooth animation.

Multipliers that control the animation speed of different layers (see the second argument of all `set_background_uv()` calls) are selected arbitrarily to create the desired parallax effect. This is purely cosmetic; go ahead and change them to witness the effect it has on the animation.

The background is now complete, and the next thing on our list is making pipes.

Making pipes

A pipe is divided into two parts, lower and upper, with a gap in between for player to pass through. Each part, in turn, consists of variable-length body and the pipe cap, or *pcap*—a fixed-size thickening at the end of the pipe facing the gap. We are going to use the following images to draw pipes:

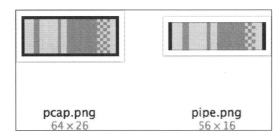

pcap.png
64 × 26

pipe.png
56 × 16

Images for pipes

If the preceding explanation doesn't ring the bell, see the first illustration in this chapter and you'll immediately understand what this means.

Again, the layout in the `kivybird.kv` file provides a convenient starting point:

```
<Pipe>:
    canvas:
        Rectangle:
            pos: (self.x + 4, self.FLOOR)
            size: (56, self.lower_len)
            texture: self.tx_pipe
            tex_coords: self.lower_coords

        Rectangle:
            pos: (self.x, self.FLOOR + self.lower_len)
            size: (64, self.PCAP_HEIGHT)
            texture: self.tx_pcap

        Rectangle:
            pos: (self.x + 4, self.upper_y)
```

```
        size: (56, self.upper_len)
        texture: self.tx_pipe
        tex_coords: self.upper_coords

    Rectangle:
        pos: (self.x, self.upper_y - self.PCAP_HEIGHT)
        size: (64, self.PCAP_HEIGHT)
        texture: self.tx_pcap

size_hint: (None, 1)
width: 64
```

Conceptually, this is very simple: four rectangles are being rendered on canvas, listed in the order of appearance in the source:

- Lower pipe body
- Lower pipe cap
- Upper pipe body
- Upper pipe cap

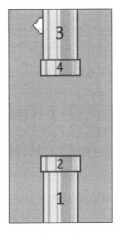

Composition of pipes from rectangles

This listing depends on many attributes of the `Pipe` object; similar to how the `Background` widget is implemented, these properties are used to connect the Python implementation of an algorithm to a graphical representation of the widget (canvas instructions).

An overview of the pipe properties

All the interesting attributes of the `Pipe` widget are shown in the following code snippet:

```python
from kivy.properties import (AliasProperty,
                             ListProperty,
                             NumericProperty,
                             ObjectProperty)

class Pipe(BaseWidget):
    FLOOR = 96
    PCAP_HEIGHT = 26
    PIPE_GAP = 120

    tx_pipe = ObjectProperty(None)
    tx_pcap = ObjectProperty(None)

    ratio = NumericProperty(0.5)
    lower_len = NumericProperty(0)
    lower_coords = ListProperty((0, 0, 1, 0, 1, 1, 0, 1))
    upper_len = NumericProperty(0)
    upper_coords = ListProperty((0, 0, 1, 0, 1, 1, 0, 1))

    upper_y = AliasProperty(
        lambda self: self.height - self.upper_len,
        None, bind=['height', 'upper_len'])
```

First, constants are set in ALL_CAPS:

- FLOOR: This is the ground level (height of the floor texture)
- PCAP_HEIGHT: This is the height of a pipe cap, also derived from the corresponding texture
- PIPE_GAP: This is the size of passage left for the player

Next come the texture properties `tx_pipe` and `tx_pcap`. They are used in the same fashion as those found in the `Background` class:

```python
class Pipe(BaseWidget):
    def __init__(self, **kwargs):
        super(Pipe, self).__init__(**kwargs)

        for name in ('pipe', 'pcap'):
            self.load_tileable(name)
```

The `ratio` property indicates where the gap is located: the value of `0.5` (the default) means center, `0` is the bottom of the screen (on the ground), and `1` is the top of the screen (in the sky).

The `lower_len` and `upper_len` properties represent pipe lengths, excluding the cap. These are derived from `ratio` and the available screen height.

The `upper_y` alias is a helper introduced to reduce typing; it's computed on the fly and is always equal to `height - upper_len` (see the implementation).

This leaves us with two important properties used to set texture coordinates for canvas instructions, namely `lower_coords` and `upper_coords`.

Setting texture coordinates

In the implementation of the `Background` widget, we were tweaking the texture's own attributes, such as `uvsize` and `uvpos`, to control its rendering. The problem with this approach is that it affects all instances of the texture.

This is perfectly fine as long as textures aren't reused on different geometries, which is exactly the case with the background. This time around, however, we need to control texture coordinates per canvas primitive, so we're not going to touch `uvsize` and `uvpos` at all. Instead, we will use `Rectangle.tex_coords`.

The `Rectangle.tex_coords` property accepts a list or tuple of eight numbers, assigning texture coordinates to corners of the rectangle in question. The mapping of coordinates to indices in the `tex_coords` list is shown in the following screenshot:

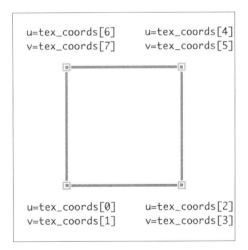

Mapping of texture coordinates to a rectangular polygon

Texture mapping commonly uses *u* and *v* variables instead of *x* and *y*. This makes it easier to tell apart geometry and texture coordinates, which are often interleaved in code.

Implementing pipes

This whole topic may sound confusing at first, so let's simplify things a bit: we're only going to fix tiling on pipes vertically, and we just need to adjust the fifth and seventh elements of `tex_coords` to achieve our noble goal. Moreover, the values in `tex_coords` have the same meaning as those in `uvsize`.

Long story short, the following function adjusts the coordinates for correct tiling based on pipe length:

```python
def set_coords(self, coords, len):
    len /= 16  # height of the texture
    coords[5:] = (len, 0, len)  # set the last 3 items
```

Easy, right? What's left to do is a boring, yet also not at all complicated math: computing the length of pipes based on `ratio` and screen height. The code is as follows:

```python
def on_size(self, *args):
    pipes_length = self.height - (
        Pipe.FLOOR + Pipe.PIPE_GAP + 2 * Pipe.PCAP_HEIGHT)
    self.lower_len = self.ratio * pipes_length
    self.upper_len = pipes_length - self.lower_len
    self.set_coords(self.lower_coords, self.lower_len)
    self.set_coords(self.upper_coords, self.upper_len)
```

This pretty self-evident code lives in the `on_size()` handler to keep all related properties in sync with the screen size. To also reflect changes to `ratio`, we can issue the following function call:

```python
self.bind(ratio=self.on_size)
```

You may have noticed that we don't change this property in our code yet. This is because the whole lifecycle of the pipes will be handled by the application class, `KivyBirdApp`, as you will see shortly.

Spawning pipes

It turns out that to create an illusion of an endless forest of pipes, we need just a screenful of them, as we can recycle ones that went off the screen and push them to the back of the queue.

We're going to create pipes about half screen width apart from one another to give the player some wiggle room; this means that only three pipes can be seen on the screen at the same time. We will create four of them for a good measure.

The following code snippet contains an implementation of the described algorithm:

```
class KivyBirdApp(App):
    pipes = []

    def on_start(self):
        self.spacing = 0.5 * self.root.width
        # ...

    def spawn_pipes(self):
        for p in self.pipes:
            self.root.remove_widget(p)

        self.pipes = []

        for i in range(4):
            p = Pipe(x=self.root.width + (self.spacing * i))
            p.ratio = random.uniform(0.25, 0.75)
            self.root.add_widget(p)
            self.pipes.append(p)
```

The use of the `pipes` list should be considered an implementation detail. We could have traversed the list of child widgets to access pipes, but it's just nicer this way.

The cleanup code at the beginning of the `spawn_pipes()` method will allow us to easily restart the game later.

We also randomize each pipe's `ratio` in this function. Notice that the range is artificially constrained to [0.25, 0.75], while technically it's [0, 1]—narrowing this space makes the game somewhat easier to play, with fewer vertical maneuvers necessary to go from gate to gate.

Moving and recycling pipes

Unlike the background where we shifted the textures' `uvpos` attribute to imitate movement, pipes actually move. This is the revised `KivyBirdApp.update()` method that involves repositioning and recycling pipes:

```
def update(self, nap):
    self.background.update(nap)

    for p in self.pipes:
        p.x -= 96 * nap
        if p.x <= -64:  # pipe gone off screen
            p.x += 4 * self.spacing
            p.ratio = random.uniform(0.25, 0.75)
```

As with the previous animations, 96 is an ad hoc time multiplier that just happens to work; increasing it makes the game more fast-paced.

When pushing back a pipe, we randomize its `ratio` again, creating a unique path for the player to follow. The following screenshot summarizes the endlessly looping result so far:

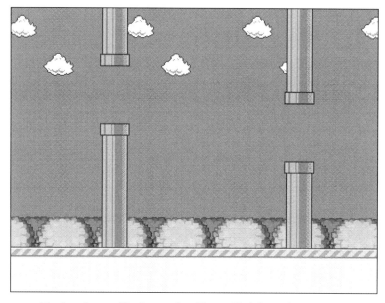

Moving pipes and background – a Flappy Bird-themed screensaver

Introducing Kivy Bird

Next on our list is the playable character, that is, the biologically improbable
Kivy Bird:

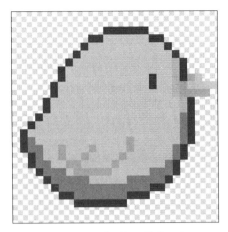

Rare species, the Kivy Bird sprite

There will be nothing fancy related to textures this time; in fact, the Bird class will
be derived from Kivy's Image widget (kivy.uix.image.Image) to completely avoid
doing any clever rendering whatsoever.

In kivybird.kv we need a bare minimum of properties involving the bird image
depicted earlier; its initial position and size are given as follows:

```
Bird:
    id: bird
    pos_hint: {'center_x': 0.3333, 'center_y': 0.6}
    size: (54, 54)
    size_hint: (None, None)
    source: 'bird.png'
```

This is the initial implementation of the Bird class in Python:

```
from kivy.uix.image import Image as ImageWidget


class Bird(ImageWidget):
    pass
```

Yup, it does nothing at all. Soon, we're going to spoil it by adding rudimentary
physics and other things, but first we need to lay some groundwork in the
application class in order to make the game stateful.

Revised application flow

Now, we shall mimic the original game somewhat:

1. At first, we'll just show the bird sitting there without any pipes or gravitation. Such a state will be denoted by `playing = False` in the code.

2. As soon as the user interacts with the game (either clicks or taps anywhere on the screen, or presses the space bar on the keyboard), the state changes to `playing = True`, pipes start spawning, and gravity starts to affect the bird, which falls as a rock to an imaginary death. The user needs to continue interacting with the game to keep the bird airborne.

3. In the event of collision with something, the game goes back to `playing = False` and everything sits in place until the next user interaction, which in turn restarts the process from step 2.

In order to implement this, we need to receive user input. Thankfully, this is borderline trivial, especially since we're interested just in the fact that an event occurred (we aren't checking where the click or tap landed, for example — the whole screen is one big button for the purposes of this game).

Accepting user input

Let's take a look at the implementation right away, since there is very little left to discuss on this particular topic:

```python
from kivy.core.window import Window, Keyboard

class KivyBirdApp(App):
    playing = False

    def on_start(self):
        # ...
        Window.bind(on_key_down=self.on_key_down)
        self.background.on_touch_down = self.user_action

    def on_key_down(self, window, key, *args):
        if key == Keyboard.keycodes['spacebar']:
            self.user_action()

    def user_action(self, *args):
        if not self.playing:
            self.spawn_pipes()
            self.playing = True
```

This is the whole user input handling we're going to need: the `on_key_down` event handles the keyboard input, checking for a specific key (in this case, the spacebar). The `on_touch_down` event handles the rest—clicking, tapping, and whatnot. Both ultimately end up calling the `user_action()` method, which in turn runs `spawn_pipes()` and sets `playing` to `True` (only when needed).

Learning to fly straight down

Next, we're going to implement gravity so that our bird could fly in at least one direction. For this, we will introduce a new `Bird.speed` property and a new constant—the acceleration of free fall. The speed vector will grow downwards each frame, resulting in a uniformly accelerated animation of falling.

The following listing contains the implementation of a described shooting bird:

```
class Bird(ImageWidget):
    ACCEL_FALL = 0.25

    speed = NumericProperty(0)

    def gravity_on(self, height):
        # Replace pos_hint with a value
        self.pos_hint.pop('center_y', None)
        self.center_y = 0.6 * height

    def update(self, nap):
        self.speed -= Bird.ACCEL_FALL
        self.y += self.speed
```

The `gravity_on()` method will be called when `playing` becomes `True`. Insert the highlighted line into the `KivyBirdApp.user_action()` method:

```
if not self.playing:
    self.bird.gravity_on(self.root.height)
    self.spawn_pipes()
    self.playing = True
```

This method effectively resets the initial position of a bird and allows vertical motion by removing the `'center_y'` constraint from `pos_hint`.

The `self.bird` reference is similar to `self.background` that we've seen earlier. The following code snippet should reside in the `KivyBirdApp.on_start()` method:

```
self.background = self.root.ids.background
self.bird = self.root.ids.bird
```

This is done for convenience alone.

We also need to call `Bird.update()` from `KivyBirdApp.update()`. At the same time, this is the perfect opportunity to put a guard preventing useless updates to game objects while not playing:

```
def update(self, nap):
    self.background.update(nap)
    if not self.playing:
        return  # don't move bird or pipes

    self.bird.update(nap)
    # rest of the code omitted
```

As you can see, the `Background.update()` method gets called no matter what; everything else is invoked only when necessary.

What's missing from this implementation is the ability to stay in the air. This will be our next topic.

Remaining in flight

Implementing the Flappy Bird-style jumpy flight is incredibly easy. We can just override the `Bird.speed` momentarily, setting it to a positive value and then letting it decay normally as the bird continues to fall. Let's add the following method to the `Bird` class:

```
ACCEL_JUMP = 5

def bump(self):
    self.speed = Bird.ACCEL_JUMP
```

Now we need to put a call to `self.bird.bump()` at the end of the `KivyBirdApp.user_action()` function, and there, all done: we can stay in the air by mashing the spacebar or clicking inside the viewport repeatedly.

Rotating the bird

Rotating the bird is a brief topic and isn't related to the physics of the bird, but instead focuses on the eye candy. It would be nice if the bird would rotate accordingly to its trajectory: if it's going up, its nose should point in a general direction of the top-right corner of the screen and towards the bottom-right corner when it declines.

The easiest way to approximate the angle is by using the value of `Bird.speed` instead:

```
class Bird(ImageWidget):
    speed = NumericProperty(0)
    angle = AliasProperty(
        lambda self: 5 * self.speed,
        None, bind=['speed'])
```

Again, the multiplier shown here is completely arbitrary.

Now, in order to actually rotate the sprite, we can introduce the following definition to the `kivybird.kv` file:

```
<Bird>:
    canvas.before:
        PushMatrix
        Rotate:
            angle: root.angle
            axis: (0, 0, 1)
            origin: root.center

    canvas.after:
        PopMatrix
```

This operation changes the local coordinate system that OpenGL uses for this sprite, potentially affecting all subsequent rendering. Don't forget to save (`PushMatrix`) and restore (`PopMatrix`) the coordinate system state; otherwise, catastrophic glitches may occur, and the whole scene can end up skewed or spinning.

> The opposite is also true: if you're experiencing inexplicable application-wide rendering problems, look for low-level OpenGL instructions that aren't properly scoped.

After these changes, the bird should properly align itself with the trajectory of the flight.

Collision detection

The last thing that is absolutely vital for the gameplay is the collision detection, which ends the game when the bird collides with either the floor, the ceiling, or a pipe.

Checking whether we've met floor or ceiling is as simple as comparing `bird.y` to a ground level or screen height (taking into account the height of the bird itself in the second comparison). In `KivyBirdApp`, we have the following code

```
def test_game_over(self):
    if self.bird.y < 90 or \
            self.bird.y > self.root.height - 50:
        return True


    return False
```

It's a bit more complex when looking for a collision with pipes, but not substantially so. We can subdivide this next check in two: first, we test for a horizontal collision using Kivy's built-in `collide_widget()` method, and then check whether vertical coordinates are within limits imposed by the `lower_len` and `upper_len` attributes of a pipe we're flying into.

Hence, the revised version of the `KivyBirdApp.test_game_over()` method is shown as follows:

```
def test_game_over(self):
    screen_height = self.root.height

    if self.bird.y < 90 or \
            self.bird.y > screen_height - 50:
        return True

    for p in self.pipes:
        if not p.collide_widget(self.bird):
            continue

        # The gap between pipes
        if (self.bird.y < p.lower_len + 116 or
            self.bird.y > screen_height - (
                p.upper_len + 75)):
            return True

    return False
```

This function returns `False` only if every check failed. This could be further optimized to test a maximum of one pipe at a time (the one which is roughly in the same area on screen as the bird; there is always at most one such pipe, given enough spacing between them).

Game over

So what happens when a collision was indeed found? As it turns out, very little; we just switch `self.playing` to `False`, and that's it. The check can be added to the bottom of `KivyBirdApp.update()` after all other computations take place:

```python
def update(self, nap):
    # ...
    if self.test_game_over():
        self.playing = False
```

This stops the world until the user triggers another interaction, restarting the game. The most rewarding part of writing the collision detection code is playtesting it, triggering the game over state in a multitude of amusing ways:

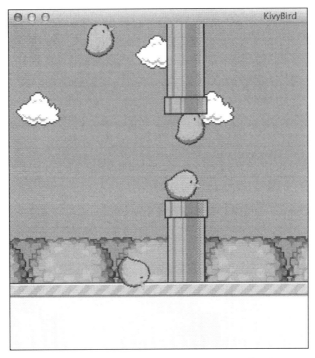

Exploring different approaches to failing (collage)

If there is no winning condition, then at least losing should be fun.

Producing sound effects

This part will be less focused on the Kivy Bird game specifically; it's more of an overview of various tools that can be employed to add sound effects to a game or application.

The biggest problem with sound effects is rarely a technical one. Creating good-quality sound effects is no small task, and software engineers oftentimes aren't skilled musicians or audio engineers. Moreover, most applications are actually usable with no sound, which is why audio can easily be purposefully neglected or just overlooked during development.

Fortunately, there are tools that facilitate producing okay-quality sound effects while possessing zero domain-specific knowledge. A perfect example is **Bfxr**, a synthesizer specifically aimed at sporadic game development. It is available for free at `www.bfxr.net`.

The usage of Bfxr family of tools boils down to clicking preset buttons until it generates a nice sound, and then hitting **Save to Disk** to store the result as a `.wav` (uncompressed sound) file.

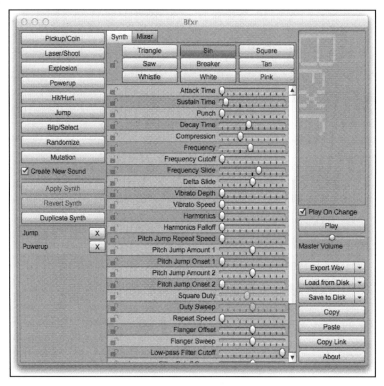

Bfxr's user interface may not seem friendly at first, but it's actually very easy to use

This is a great tool in terms of productivity. Using Bfxr, you can create passable sound effects literally within minutes—and they will be (mostly) unique to your app. For many hobbyist game developers, this program is truly a game changer, pun intended.

Kivy sound playback

On the programmatic side of things, the API for playback that Kivy provides is dead simple:

```
from kivy.core.audio import SoundLoader

snd = SoundLoader.load('sound.wav')
snd.play()
```

The `play()` method starts playback, and that's it. Well, not really: there is a slight problem with this simplistic approach, especially for games.

In many game situations, it may be desirable to play the same sound over and over in rapid succession so that samples overlap. Take, for example, automatic fire. The problem with Kivy's `Sound` class (not unique to it, however—for example, the `<audio>` tag in HTML5 behaves similarly) is that it allows only one instance of the sample to play at any given time.

The options are as follows:

- Wait until the previous playback has ended (the default behavior, all subsequent events will be silent)
- Stop and restart the playback for each event, which is also problematic (this may introduce unnecessary delays, clicks, or other audio artifacts)

To solve this issue, we need to create a pool (actually a queue) of `Sound` objects so that each subsequent call to `play()` involves another `Sound`. When the queue is exhausted, we rewind it and start from the beginning. Given a queue large enough, we can get rid of the aforementioned `Sound` limitation completely. In practice, such pool rarely exceeds a size of 10.

Let's take a look at the implementation of the described technique:

```
class MultiAudio:
    _next = 0

    def __init__(self, filename, count):
        self.buf = [SoundLoader.load(filename)
                    for i in range(count)]
```

```
def play(self):
    self.buf[self._next].play()
    self._next = (self._next + 1) % len(self.buf)
```

The usage is as follows:

```
snd = MultiAudio('sound.wav', 5)
snd.play()
```

The second argument to the constructor stands for pool size. Note how we keep rudimentary compatibility with the existing Sound API, namely the play() method. This allows using the code as a drop-in replacement of a Sound object in simple scenarios.

Adding sound to the Kivy Bird game

To finish things off with a practical example, let's add sound effects to the Kivy Bird game we've written over the course of this chapter.

There are two frequent events that could use a soundtrack, namely, the bird climbing and the bird colliding with objects and triggering the game over state.

The former event, initiated by clicking or tapping, can indeed happen very frequently in a rapid succession; we'll use a sample pool for this one. The latter, game over, can't possibly occur quite as fast, so it's fine to leave it as a plain Sound object:

```
snd_bump = MultiAudio('bump.wav', 4)
snd_game_over = SoundLoader.load('game_over.wav')
```

This code makes use of the MultiAudio class laid out earlier. The only thing left is to put calls to the play() method at the appropriate points, as shown in the following code snippet:

```
if self.test_game_over():
    snd_game_over.play()
    self.playing = False

def user_action(self, *args):
    snd_bump.play()
```

From now on, the gameplay will be accompanied by heart-rending sounds. This concludes the Kivy Bird game tutorial; I hope you liked it.

Summary

In this chapter, we made a small Kivy game from simple building blocks such as canvas instructions and widgets.

As a UI toolkit, Kivy gets many things right and its remarkable flexibility allows you to build pretty much anything, be it another boring Twitter client or a video game. One aspect that deserves special mention is Kivy's implementation of properties—these are immensely helpful to organize data flow across the board and help us to effectively eliminate useless updates (such as redraws in the absence of changed properties).

Another thing about Kivy that may be surprising and counterintuitive at first is its relatively high performance—especially since Python isn't exactly famous for being extremely quick. This is partly because low-level subsystems in Kivy are written in Cython and compiled to a blazing fast machine code, with performance levels about the same as, for example, the C language. Also, the use of hardware-accelerated graphics all but guarantees smooth animations, if done properly.

We will explore the topic of cranking up the rendering performance in the next chapter.

8
Introducing Shaders

Congratulations on making it this far! The last two chapters will somewhat stand out from the rest of the book, as we will take a completely different perspective on Kivy and dive into low-level details of the OpenGL renderer, such as the **OpenGL Shading Language** (**GLSL**). This will allow us to write high-performance code with very little overhead.

Starting from an unscientific introduction to OpenGL, we will proceed to writing a fast sprite-based engine for a starfield demonstration (basically, a screensaver) and finally, a shoot-em-up game (commonly abbreviated as just *shmup*). The code from this chapter will serve as a basis for the next one, unlike other projects in this book that were largely self-contained. We will lay the foundation here and then build upon it in the next chapter, turning a technical demo into a playable game.

This chapter attempts to cover many complex topics with a sufficient level of detail, but it is way too short to serve as an all-encompassing reference guide. In addition to this, OpenGL, as a standard, evolves very quickly, introducing new features and deprecating the obsolete stuff. So, if you notice a discrepancy between the material presented in the chapter and the objective reality, please look it up—chances are that you're living in the bright future of computing, where things have changed significantly.

It should be mentioned upfront that the approach to high-performance rendering discussed here, despite being wildly different from the regular Kivy code, for the most part stays compatible with it and can be used side by side with ordinary widgets. Therefore, it's perfectly feasible to implement only the resource-hungry parts of an app in GLSL—those that will otherwise become a performance bottleneck.

Unscientific introduction to OpenGL

This section will provide a quick introduction to the basics of OpenGL. It's next to impossible to meaningfully summarize all the nooks and crannies of the standard here; hence it is "unscientific," superficial.

OpenGL is a popular low-level graphical API. It's standardized and almost ubiquitous. Desktop and mobile operating systems commonly ship with an implementation of OpenGL (in the case of mobile, OpenGL ES, a feature-restricted subset of the standard; here, **ES** stands for **embedded systems**). Modern web browsers also implement a variant of OpenGL ES called WebGL.

Wide distribution and a well-defined compatibility makes OpenGL a good target for cross-platform apps, especially video games and graphical toolkits. Kivy also relies on OpenGL to perform rendering across all the supported platforms.

Concepts and parallelism

OpenGL operates on basic primitives such as individual vertices and pixels on screen. For example, we can feed three vertices to it and render a triangle, thus computing color for each affected pixel (depending on the pipeline described in the next image). You might have guessed that working at this level of abstraction is extremely cumbersome. This pretty much summarizes the raison d'être of high-level graphical frameworks, including Kivy: they're there to conceal the gory details of a rendering pipeline behind a more comfortable abstraction, such as working with widgets and layouts.

The low-level rendering pipeline functions as follows:

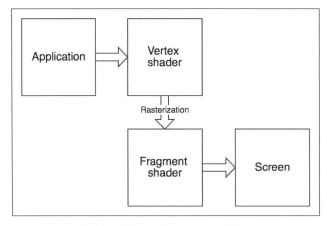

An OpenGL pipeline (oversimplified)

The complete explanation of the preceding figure is as follows:

- The application gives OpenGL an array of **vertices** (points), **indices** that allow us to reuse the points, and other arbitrary values (called **uniforms**).

- A **vertex shader** is invoked for every vertex, transforming it if needed and optionally doing other calculations. Its output is then passed to a corresponding fragment shader.

- A **fragment shader** (sometimes called **pixel shader**) is invoked for every affected pixel, computing that pixel's color. More often than not, it takes into account the vertex shader's output but might also return, for example, a constant color.

- Pixels are rendered on screen, and other bookkeeping tasks are performed; these tasks are of no interest to us at this point.

 A collection of vertices used together as a batch is commonly called a **model** or **mesh**. It is not necessarily continuous and might consist of scattered polygons as well; the rationale for such models will be mentioned shortly.

The "secret sauce" behind the blazing speed of OpenGL is its inherent massive parallelism. The functions mentioned earlier (namely, vertex and pixel shaders) might not be crazy fast by themselves, but as they are invoked simultaneously on a GPU, the delay imposed by shaders usually doesn't grow exponentially with the shaders' complexity; such growth can be close to linear on a decent hardware.

To put things in scale, given today's personal computers (at the time of writing this book), we're talking about multitasking and parallel programming with anywhere from 2 to 16 CPU cores in commodity hardware. Mid-range graphics cards, on the other hand, effectively have thousands of GPU cores; this makes them capable of running way more computations in parallel.

As a consequence though, each task runs in isolation. Unlike the threads in general-purpose programming, a shader cannot wait for the other shader's output without significantly degrading performance, except where implied by pipeline architecture (as mentioned earlier, a vertex shader passes values to a fragment shader). This restriction might be a bit mind-bending to work around as you start writing GLSL.

This is also why some algorithms can be implemented to run efficiently on GPU while others cannot. Interestingly, modern cryptography functions such as **bcrypt** are specifically designed to reduce performance of a highly parallelized implementation—this makes such functions inherently more secure by limiting the effectiveness of a brute-force attack.

Performance gains, or lack thereof

It is important to understand that there are no immediate performance gains from using raw OpenGL calls at all times; in many cases, high-level frameworks such as Kivy will do just fine. For example, when rendering a polygon somewhere on a screen, roughly the following sequence of actions takes place:

1. The geometry and position of a polygon are defined in Python.
2. The vertices, indices, and related assets (such as textures) are uploaded to the graphics driver.
3. The vertex shader is invoked. It applies the necessary transformations, including positioning, rotation, scaling, and so on.
4. Finally, the corresponding fragment shader is invoked; this results in a raster image that might be displayed on the screen.

It doesn't matter whether you use Kivy widgets for this task or stick with writing raw OpenGL commands and GLSL shaders—both the performance and result will likely be the same, with negligible differences at best. This is because Kivy runs very similar OpenGL code behind the scenes.

In other words, this example bears very little potential for low-level optimization, and this is exactly the reason why a game such as *Kivy Bird*, consisting of scarce rectangles and very little else, should be implemented at the highest level of abstraction available. Basically, we could have optimized away the creation of a widget or two in Kivy Bird, but this is hardly even measurable.

Improving performance

So, how do we actually boost performance? The answer is, by reducing the amount of work done on the Python side of things and batching similar objects together for rendering.

Let's consider the scenario where we need to render over 9,000 similar polygons (a particle system, for example, autumn leaves scattered on the ground or a cluster of stars in space).

If we use Kivy widgets for individual polygons, we're creating a large number of Python objects that exist solely for the purpose of serializing themselves to OpenGL instructions. Moreover, each widget has its own set of vertices that it feeds to the graphics driver, thus issuing excessive API calls and creating a lot of distinct (yet very similar) meshes.

Manually, we're able to, at the very least, do the following:

- Avoid the instantiation of many Python classes and just keep all the coordinates in an array. If we store them in a format suitable for direct OpenGL consumption, there is no need for the serialization step.

- Lump all geometry together as a single model and thus make much less API calls. Batching is always a nice optimization, as it allows OpenGL to do a better job at the parallel execution of things.

We will implement the described approach by the end of this chapter.

Taking a closer look at GLSL

As a language, GLSL is closely related to C; in particular, syntactically, they're very similar. GLSL is strongly, statically typed (more so than C).

If you aren't familiar with the C syntax, here's a very quick primer. First of all, unlike Python, in C-like languages, indentation is insignificant, and ending statements with a semicolon is mandatory. Logical blocks are enclosed in curly braces.

GLSL supports both C and C++ style comments:

```
/* ANSI C-style comment */
// C++ one-line comment
```

Variable declarations are in the `[type] [name] [= optional value];` format:

```
float a; // this has no direct Python equivalent
int b = 1;
```

Functions are defined using the `[type] [name] ([arguments]) { [body of function] }` syntax:

```
float pow2(float x)
{
    return x * x;
}
```

Control structures are written like this:

```
if (x < 9.0)
{
    x = 9.0;
}
```

That's it for the most part; you should be able to read the GLSL code now, regardless of whether you have a background in C programming or not.

The entry point of a shader is designated by a `main()` function. In the following code, we'll put both vertex and fragment shaders together in one file; so, there will be two `main()` functions per file. This is how these functions look:

```
void main(void)
{
    // code
}
```

A special `void` type means absence of value, and unlike Python's `NoneType`, you cannot declare a variable of type `void`. In the case of the preceding `main()` function, both the return value and arguments are omitted; hence the function's declaration reads `void main(void)`. Instead of returning the result of a computation from the function, shaders write it to special built-in variables, `gl_Position`, `gl_FragColor`, and others, depending on the shader type and the desired effect. This also holds true for input parameters.

A GLSL type system closely reflects its usage domain. Unlike C, it has highly specialized types for vectors and matrices; these types support mathematical operations on them (so, you can multiply matrices with just the `mat1 * mat2` syntax; how cool is that!). In computer graphics, matrices are commonly used to mess with the coordinate system, as you will see shortly.

In the next section, we'll write a couple of simple GLSL shaders to demonstrate some of the concepts discussed earlier.

Using custom shaders in Kivy

Apart from GLSL, we also need to have the usual Python code that initializes the window, loads shaders, and so on. The following program will serve as a good starting point:

```python
from kivy.app import App
from kivy.base import EventLoop
from kivy.graphics import Mesh
from kivy.graphics.instructions import RenderContext
from kivy.uix.widget import Widget

class GlslDemo(Widget):
    def __init__(self, **kwargs):
        Widget.__init__(self, **kwargs)
        self.canvas = RenderContext(use_parent_projection=True)
        self.canvas.shader.source = 'basic.glsl'
        # Set up geometry here.
```

```
class GlslApp(App):
    def build(self):
        EventLoop.ensure_window()
        return GlslDemo()

if __name__ == '__main__':
    GlslApp().run()
```

We created just one widget named `GlslDemo` in this example; it will host all the rendering. `RenderContext` is a customizable `Canvas` subclass that allows us to replace shaders easily, as shown in the listing. The `basic.glsl` file contains both vertex and fragment shaders; we will get to it in a minute.

Note that this time, we aren't using the Kivy language at all, because no layout hierarchy is planned, so there is no accompanying `glsl.kv` file. Instead, we will designate the root widget manually by returning it from the `GlslApp.build()` method.

The call to `EventLoop.ensure_window()` is needed, because we want to be able to access OpenGL features, such as the GLSL compiler, while running `GlslDemo.__init__()`. If there is still no application window (and more importantly, no corresponding OpenGL context) at that point in time, the program will crash.

Building the geometry

Before we begin writing shaders, we need something to render—a series of vertices, that is, a model. We'll stick with a simple rectangle that consists of two right triangles with a common hypotenuse (the subdivision is because baseline polygons are essentially triangular).

> Kivy, albeit two-dimensional for the most part, does not impose this limitation in any way. OpenGL, on the other hand, is inherently three-dimensional, so you can use realistic models seamlessly to create modern-looking games, and even mix them with regular Kivy widgets for UI (in-game menus and so on). This possibility is not further detailed in the book, but the underlying mechanics are just the same as described here.

This is the updated `__init__()` method of the `GlslDemo` widget, with an explanation following it:

```
def __init__(self, **kwargs):
    Widget.__init__(self, **kwargs)
    self.canvas = RenderContext(use_parent_projection=True)
```

```
        self.canvas.shader.source = 'basic.glsl'

        fmt = (   # Step 1
            (b'vPosition', 2, 'float'),
        )

        vertices = (   # Step 2
            0,    0,
            255, 0,
            255, 255,
            0,    255,
        )

        indices = (0, 1, 2, 2, 3, 0)   # Step 3

        with self.canvas:
            Mesh(fmt=fmt, mode='triangles',   # Step 4
                indices=indices, vertices=vertices)
```

Let's walk through this function, because it's essential to understand it correctly before moving on to more complex things:

- When writing code that makes use of OpenGL, the first thing you'll notice is that there is no built-in standard format for vertices that we need to adhere to; instead, we need to define such a format ourselves. In the simplest case, we need just the position of each vertex; this is called `vPosition`. Our rectangle is two-dimensional, so we'll pass just two coordinates, which are floating point by default. Hence, we get the resulting line `(b'vPosition', 2, 'float')`.

- Now that we have decided on the format of the vertices, it's time to put these vertices in an array that will soon be handed over to the renderer. This is exactly what the `vertices = (...)` line does. It's important that the tuple is flat and unstructured. We will define the record format separately and then pack all the values tightly together, without field delimiters and the like—all in the name of efficiency. This is also how C structs typically work.

- Indices are needed to duplicate (reuse) vertices. More often than not, a vertex is used in more than one triangle. Instead of repeating it literally in the array of vertices, we resort to repeating its index in the array of indices—it's typically smaller, so the whole thing ends up taking less memory, proportional to the size of an individual vertex. See the next section for a more detailed explanation of indices.

- With all the required data structures in place, we can finally assemble the mesh using the homonymous Kivy canvas instruction, `Mesh`. Now, it will be rendered over the course of normal widget rendering, which has a nice side effect of composability with other Kivy widgets. Our GLSL code can be effortlessly used in conjunction with all the previous developments. This is certainly a good thing.

> Throughout this chapter, we have used the word *array* in a C sense—a continuous memory region containing homogeneous data. This is only tentatively related to the Python data structure having the same name; in fact, on the Python side of things, we're mostly using tuples or lists as a substitute.

Illustrating the Indices

To explain OpenGL indices better, let's visualize our example. These are our vertices from the preceding sample code, in the format of (x, y):

```
vertices = (
    0,    0,
    255, 0,
    255, 255,
    0,    255,
)
```

An index is just that—a serial number of a vertex in the `vertices` list, and it is zero-based. The following figure illustrates the assignment of indices to the vertices in this setup:

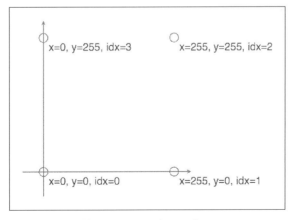

Vertices scattered on a plane

Right now, the vertices aren't connected, so they form a point cloud at best, not a structured polygonal shape. To fix this, we need to specify the `indices` list—it will group the existing vertices into triangles. Its definition, again taken from the sample code, is as follows:

```
indices = (
    0, 1, 2,  # Three vertices make a triangle.
    2, 3, 0,  # And another one.
)
```

We've built two triangles here: the first one consists of vertices 0 to 2, and the second one out of vertices 2, 3, and 0. Note how the 0th and 2nd vertices are reused.

This is illustrated in the following figure. Never mind the colors; they are strictly explanatory and not "real" colors yet. We'll get to coloring things on the screen shortly.

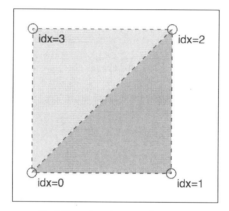

Building triangles out of vertices

This pretty much summarizes the utility and usage of indices in OpenGL-related code.

> The tendency of optimizing in-memory sizes of data structures in OpenGL has very little to do with saving RAM per se—the video card interface throughput is a more serious bottleneck in most scenarios, so we're aiming at passing more stuff per frame, not just compressing data for the sake of economy. This distinction, while very important, makes no difference early on.

Writing GLSL

This is where things will get more interesting. In a moment, we'll be writing GLSL code that executes on a GPU. As we've already mentioned, it's C-like and crazy fast.

Let's start with the basics. Kivy expects that both the vertex and the fragment shaders live in the same file, delimited using a special syntax, `'---vertex'` and `'---fragment'` (shown in the next code snippet). It's important to stress out that both these delimiters and the `$HEADER$` syntax are specific to Kivy; they are not part of any standard, and you won't see them elsewhere.

This is how the boilerplate for a typical Kivy shader file looks:

```
---vertex
$HEADER$

void main(void)
{
    // vertex shader
    gl_Position = ...
}


---fragment
$HEADER$

void main(void)
{
    // fragment shader
    gl_FragColor = ...
}
```

Henceforth, we'll omit most of the boilerplate code to shorten listings—but keep in mind that it's always assumed to be there; otherwise, things might not work as expected, or not at all.

The `$HEADER$` macro is context-sensitive and means different things depending on the type of shader.

Inside a vertex shader, `$HEADER$` is a shortcut for roughly the following code:

```
varying vec4 frag_color;
varying vec2 tex_coord0;

attribute vec2 vPosition;
attribute vec2 vTexCoords0;

uniform mat4   modelview_mat;
uniform mat4   projection_mat;
uniform vec4   color;
uniform float opacity;
```

In a fragment shader, $HEADER$ expands to the following code:

```
varying vec4 frag_color;
varying vec2 tex_coord0;

uniform sampler2D texture0;
```

(Some not very important bits have been redacted for clarity.)

Clearly, these might be subject to change in future versions of Kivy.

Storage classes and types

In the previous code, variables are annotated not only with a type, but also with a storage qualifier. Here is a quick rundown of both:

Storage classes	
attribute	This denotes the properties of vertices as specified by the vertex format. Attributes are passed from an application.
uniform	Uniforms are global variables at the GLSL level. They are also passed from an application, but unlike attributes these do not vary with each vertex.
varying	These are variables passed from the vertex shader to the fragment shader.
Commonly used data types	
float	This is the scalar floating-point variable type, similar to other languages.
vec2, vec3, vec4	This is a tuple of length 2, 3, and 4; it contains floats. It might represent points, colors, and so on.
mat2, mat3, mat4	These refer to matrices of sizes 2×2, 3×3, 4×4, respectively.
sampler2D	This represents a texture that allows lookups (getting the color from specified coordinates).

Basic shaders

Now, without further preliminaries, let's write our first and simplest shaders that do nothing special.

The default-like vertex shader reads:

```
void main(void)
{
    vec4 pos = vec4(vPosition.xy, 0.0, 1.0);
    gl_Position = projection_mat * modelview_mat * pos;
}
```

This transforms the location of each vertex into Kivy's preferred coordinate system, with the origin at the lower-left corner.

> We will not attempt to describe the nuances of the transformation of coordinates here, as the topic is way too complex for an entry-level tutorial. Moreover, it isn't even necessary to fully understand this code, or to finish reading the book.
>
> If you're interested in a more comprehensive description of the topic, a nice short summary of the OpenGL coordinate space and the use of matrices can be found at http://www.learnopengles.com/understanding-opengls-matrices/.

The easiest fragment shader is a function that returns a constant color:

```
void main(void)
{
    gl_FragColor = vec4(1.0, 0.0, 0.5, 1.0);
}
```

This outputs an RGBA color equal to #FF007F for every pixel.

If you run the program now, you would see output similar to the following screenshot:

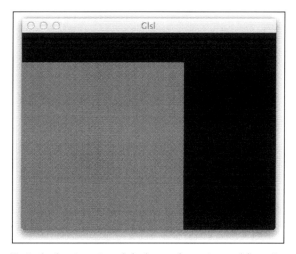

Basic shaders in action: default transformation and flat color

Finally, we have a visible result of our ordeal. It isn't particularly interesting right now, but it is still better than nothing. Let's fiddle with it and see where this takes us.

Procedural coloring

Another lazy way to compute color, apart from always returning the same value, is to derive it from something that is immediately available in a corresponding shader, for example, fragment coordinates.

Let's assume that we want to compute each pixel's RGB color as follows:

- The R channel will be proportional to the *x* coordinate
- The G channel will be proportional to the *y* coordinate
- B will be an average of R and G.

This simple algorithm can be easily implemented in a fragment shader as follows:

```
void main(void)
{
    float r = gl_FragCoord.x / 255.0;
    float g = gl_FragCoord.y / 255.0;
    float b = 0.5 * (r + g);
    gl_FragColor = vec4(r, g, b, 1.0);
}
```

The gl_FragCoord built-in variable contains fragment coordinates (not necessarily representing a whole physical pixel) relative to the application window. A division by 255.0 — the size of the mesh, inlined for simplicity — is necessary to put color components in the range of [0...1].

This replaces the previously seen flat color with a gradient as follows:

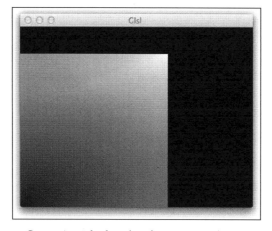

Computing color based on fragment coordinates

Colorful vertices

A similar effect can be made data-driven by giving vertices their own colors. For this, we need to expand the vertex format to contain another per-vertex attribute, vColor. In Python code, this amounts to the following definition:

```python
fmt = (
    (b'vPosition', 2, 'float'),
    (b'vColor', 3, 'float'),
)

vertices = (
    0,    0,    0.462, 0.839, 1,
    255,  0,    0.831, 0.984, 0.474,
    255,  255,  1,     0.541, 0.847,
    0,    255,  1,     0.988, 0.474,
)

indices = (0, 1, 2, 2, 3, 0)
```

With an updated format, a vertex now consists of five floats, up from two. It's crucial to keep the vertices list in sync with the format; otherwise, weird things will happen.

As per our declaration, vColor is an RGB color, and for a vertex shader, we ultimately need RGBA. Instead of passing a constant alpha channel for each vertex, we'll pad it in the vertex shader, similar to how we expand vPosition from vec2 to vec4.

This is what our revised vertex shader looks like:

```glsl
attribute vec3 vColor;

void main(void)
{
    frag_color = vec4(vColor.rgb, 1.0);
    vec4 pos = vec4(vPosition.xy, 0.0, 1.0);
    gl_Position = projection_mat * modelview_mat * pos;
}
```

. . .

GLSL notations such as vColor.rgb and vPosition.xy are called *swizzling*. They can be used to efficiently manipulate parts of a vector, similar in concept to Python slices.

By itself, vColor.rgb simply means "take the first three vector components;" in Python code, we would write vColor[:3]. It's also possible to, for example, reverse the order of the color channels easily using vColor.bgr, or take just one channel using vColor.ggg (this will turn the resulting picture into grayscale).

Up to four vector components can be addressed in this fashion, using either .xyzw, .rgba, or a more obscure .stpq notation; they all do exactly the same thing.

Having done this, the fragment shader becomes very simple:

```
void main(void)
{
    gl_FragColor = frag_color;
}
```

Interestingly enough, we get color interpolation between vertices for free, resulting in a smooth gradient; this is how OpenGL works. The next screenshot depicts the output of the program:

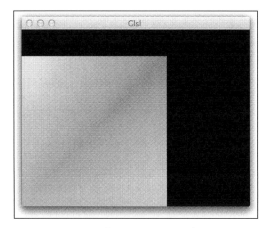

Passing color as a vertex attribute

Texture mapping

To wrap up this series of simple demos, let's apply a texture to our rectangle. Once again, we need to expand the definition of a vertex format, this time, to assign texture coordinates to each vertex:

```
fmt = (
    (b'vPosition', 2, 'float'),
    (b'vTexCoords0', 2, 'float'),
)

vertices = (
    0,   0,    0, 1,
    255, 0,    1, 1,
    255, 255,  1, 0,
    0,   255,  0, 0,
)
```

Texture coordinates are usually in the [0...1] range, with the origin in the upper-left corner—note that this is different from the default Kivy's coordinate system. If, at some point, you see a texture flipped upside down for no apparent reason, check the texture coordinates first—they're likely the culprit.

One more thing that we need to take care of on the Python side of things is loading the texture and passing it to renderer. This is how it's done:

```
from kivy.core.image import Image

with self.canvas:
    Mesh(fmt=fmt, mode='triangles',
         indices=indices, vertices=vertices,
         texture=Image('kivy.png').texture)
```

This will load a file named `kivy.png` from the current directory and convert it into a usable texture. For the sake of demonstration, we will use the following image:

The texture used for the demo

As for the shaders, they aren't very different from the previous iteration. The vertex shader simply passes texture coordinates through, untouched:

```
void main(void)
{
    tex_coord0 = vTexCoords0;
    vec4 pos = vec4(vPosition.xy, 0.0, 1.0);
    gl_Position = projection_mat * modelview_mat * pos;
}
```

The fragment shader uses the interpolated `tex_coord0` coordinates to perform a lookup on the `texture0` texture, thus returning the corresponding color:

```
void main(void)
{
    gl_FragColor = texture2D(texture0, tex_coord0);
}
```

When put together, our code delivers the expected result:

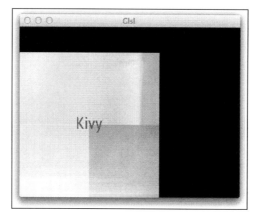

Simple GLSL texture mapping

To summarize, this introduction to shaders should have given you enough courage to try to write your own small shader-based programs. Most importantly, don't feel intimidated if certain things don't make much sense—GLSL is a complex subject, and learning it systematically is not a small endeavor.

It pays off, however, in giving you a much better understanding of how things work under the hood. Even if you don't write low-level code on a daily basis, you can still use this knowledge to identify and avoid performance bottlenecks and generally improve the architecture of your applications.

Making the Starfield app

Armed with our newfound knowledge of GLSL, let's build a starfield screensaver, that is, a non-interactive demonstration of stars fleeing from the center of the screen to its sides, under the influence of an imaginary centrifugal force or something.

 As dynamic visual effects are hard to describe unequivocally and screenshots aren't very helpful in this regard either, run the code that accompanies the chapter to get a better idea of what's going on.

Conceptually, each star goes through the same action sequence:

1. It spawns randomly near the center of the screen.
2. The star moves in the opposite direction from the screen center until it's no longer visible.
3. Then it respawns, going back to square one.

We will also make stars accelerate and grow in size as they approach the edges of the screen to simulate the faux depth.

The following screenshot attempts (or, to be more specific, fails due to the highly dynamic nature of the demo) to illustrate what the end result will look like:

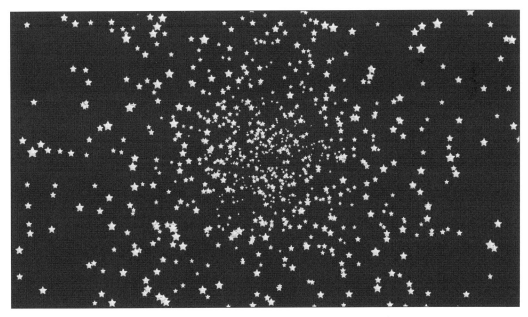

A screenshot cannot convey the motion sickness, but it's there

Application structure

The new application class bears a striking resemblance to what we did earlier in this chapter. Similar to the examples discussed earlier, we aren't using the Kivy language to describe the (non-existent) widget hierarchy, so there is no `starfield.kv` file.

The class consists of two methods, which are shown here:

```
from kivy.base import EventLoop
from kivy.clock import Clock

class StarfieldApp(App):
    def build(self):
        EventLoop.ensure_window()
        return Starfield()

    def on_start(self):
        Clock.schedule_interval(self.root.update_glsl,
                                60 ** -1)
```

The `build()` method creates and returns the root widget, `Starfield`; it will be in charge of all the math and rendering—basically, everything that happens throughout the application.

The `on_start()` handler tells the aforementioned root widget to update 60 times per second by calling its `update_glsl()` method after the application has been started.

The `Starfield` class is also split in two: there is the usual `__init__()` method, which is responsible for the creation of the data structures, and the `update_glsl()` method, which advances the scene (calculates an updated position of each star) and renders stars on the screen.

Data structures and initializers

Let's now review the initialization code:

```
from kivy.core.image import Image
from kivy.graphics.instructions import RenderContext
from kivy.uix.widget import Widget

NSTARS = 1000

class Starfield(Widget):
    def __init__(self, **kwargs):
        Widget.__init__(self, **kwargs)
```

```
self.canvas = RenderContext(use_parent_projection=True)
self.canvas.shader.source = 'starfield.glsl'

self.vfmt = (
    (b'vCenter',     2, 'float'),
    (b'vScale',      1, 'float'),
    (b'vPosition',   2, 'float'),
    (b'vTexCoords0', 2, 'float'),
)

self.vsize = sum(attr[1] for attr in self.vfmt)

self.indices = []
for i in range(0, 4 * NSTARS, 4):
    self.indices.extend((
        i, i + 1, i + 2, i + 2, i + 3, i))

self.vertices = []
for i in range(NSTARS):
    self.vertices.extend((
        0, 0, 1, -24, -24, 0, 1,
        0, 0, 1,  24, -24, 1, 1,
        0, 0, 1,  24,  24, 1, 0,
        0, 0, 1, -24,  24, 0, 0,
    ))

self.texture = Image('star.png').texture

self.stars = [Star(self, i) for i in range(NSTARS)]
```

NSTARS is the total number of stars; try raising or lowering it to alter the density of the starfield. Regarding performance, even a mediocre machine boasting a slow, integrated Intel video card easily supports thousands of stars. Any half-decent dedicated graphics hardware will handle tens of thousands of simultaneously rendered sprites with ease.

Unlike the previous examples, this time we will not fill the indices and vertices with the final, useful data right away; instead, we will prepare placeholder arrays that will be continuously updated later, as part of the update_glsl() routine.

The `vfmt` vertex format includes the following properties; a part of these has already been showcased in this chapter:

Vertex attribute	Its function
vCenter	This denotes the coordinates of the star's center point on the screen
vScale	This is the star's size factor, 1 being the original size (48 × 48 pixels)
vPosition	This is the position of each vertex relative to the star's center point
vTexCoords0	This refers to the texture coordinates

The property that we haven't mentioned yet, `vsize`, is the length of a single vertex in the array of vertices. It's computed from the vertex format as a sum of its middle column.

The `vertices` list contains nearly all data about stars that we need to retain; however, as it is flat and not implicitly structured, it's very unwieldy to operate on. This is where a helper class, `Star`, comes into play. It encapsulates the gory details of accessing and updating a selected entry in the array of vertices so that we don't have to compute offsets throughout our code.

The `Star` class also keeps track of various properties that aren't part of the vertex format, that is, polar coordinates (`angle` and `distance` from the center) and `size`, which increases with time.

This is the initialization of the `Star` class:

```python
import math
from random import random

class Star:
    angle = 0
    distance = 0
    size = 0.1

    def __init__(self, sf, i):
        self.sf = sf
        self.base_idx = 4 * i * sf.vsize
        self.reset()

    def reset(self):
        self.angle = 2 * math.pi * random()
        self.distance = 90 * random() + 10
        self.size = 0.05 * random() + 0.05
```

Here, `base_idx` is the index of this star's first vertex in the array of vertices; we also kept a reference, `sf`, to the `Starfield` instance to be able to access `vertices` later.

The `reset()` function, when called, reverts the star's attributes to default (slightly randomized) values.

Advancing the scene

The `Starfield.update_glsl()` method implements the algorithm of the starfield motion and is frequently invoked by Kivy's clock scheduled in the `on_start()` handler of the application class. Its source code is as follows:

```
from kivy.graphics import Mesh

def update_glsl(self, nap):
    x0, y0 = self.center
    max_distance = 1.1 * max(x0, y0)

    for star in self.stars:
        star.distance *= 2 * nap + 1
        star.size += 0.25 * nap

        if (star.distance > max_distance):
            star.reset()
        else:
            star.update(x0, y0)

    self.canvas.clear()

    with self.canvas:
        Mesh(fmt=self.vfmt, mode='triangles',
             indices=self.indices, vertices=self.vertices,
             texture=self.texture)
```

First off, we calculate the distance limit, `max_distance`, after which the stars respawn near the center of the screen. Then, we iterate over the list of stars, setting them in motion and enlarging them slightly on the way. Stars that have escaped the terminal distance are reset.

The final part of the function should look familiar. It's the same rendering code as seen in the preceding examples. A call to `canvas.clear()` is necessary; otherwise, a new mesh will be added on each call, swiftly bringing the overwhelmed graphics card to a grinding halt.

The last piece of Python code that hasn't been revealed is the `Star.update()` method. It refreshes the four vertices belonging to a star, writing new coordinates to appropriate places in the `vertices` array:

```
def iterate(self):
    return range(self.j,
                 self.j + 4 * self.sf.vsize,
                 self.sf.vsize)

def update(self, x0, y0):
    x = x0 + self.distance * math.cos(self.angle)
    y = y0 + self.distance * math.sin(self.angle)

    for i in self.iterate():
        self.sf.vertices[i:i + 3] = (x, y, self.size)
```

The `iterate()` helper is for convenience only and could have been inlined, but there's no such thing as superfluous readability, so let's keep it this way.

To reiterate (pun intended), this whole memory-mapping process serves a noble goal of eliminating the need to serialize our numerous objects in each frame; this helps performance.

Writing a corresponding GLSL

Shaders used in the following program are also reminiscent of what we've seen earlier; they are only a little lengthier. This is the vertex shader:

```
attribute vec2  vCenter;
attribute float vScale;

void main(void)
{
    tex_coord0 = vTexCoords0;
    mat4 move_mat = mat4
        (1.0, 0.0, 0.0, vCenter.x,
         0.0, 1.0, 0.0, vCenter.y,
         0.0, 0.0, 1.0, 0.0,
         0.0, 0.0, 0.0, 1.0);
    vec4 pos = vec4(vPosition.xy * vScale, 0.0, 1.0) * move_mat;
    gl_Position = projection_mat * modelview_mat * pos;
}
```

Simply put, we're multiplying the relative coordinates of all the vertices by a factor of vScale, which resizes the mesh proportionally, and then translating them to the position given by a vCenter attribute. The move_mat matrix is the translation matrix, an affine transformation method that you might or might not remember from your linear algebra class.

To compensate, the fragment shader is very simple:

```
void main(void)
{
    gl_FragColor = texture2D(texture0, tex_coord0);
}
```

Its ultimate purpose is to put this beautiful thing on the screen:

Star texture, zoomed in

That's it. Our starfield is now finished and ready for astronomical observation with the unaided eye (or any other usage you can think of).

Summary

This chapter aimed (and hopefully succeeded) to introduce you to a beautiful hardware-accelerated world of low-level OpenGL and GLSL development filled with vertices, indices, and shaders.

Direct programming of the GPU is an insanely powerful concept, and with this power always comes responsibility. Shaders are much harder to grasp than regular Python code; debugging might involve a fair measure of guesswork, and there is no convenient interactive environment, such as Python's REPL, to speak of. That said, there is no clear heuristic whether writing a raw GLSL would be useful for any particular application—it should be decided on a case-by-case basis.

Examples in this chapter were deliberately simple to serve as a gentle learning experience, not a test of cognitive abilities. This is mainly because GLSL programming is a very non-trivial, convoluted subject to study, with numerous books and online tutorials dedicated to mastering it, and this short chapter is by no means a comprehensive guide to all things OpenGL.

So far, we've just barely scratched the surface of what's possible. The next chapter will capitalize on the code we wrote here to do a slightly more interesting thing: create a blazing fast shoot-em-up game.

9
Making a Shoot-Em-Up Game

Welcome to the final chapter of Kivy Blueprints. In this tutorial, we're going to build a shoot-em-up game (or *shmup* for short) — a fast-paced action game about shooting things indefinitely.

This is a small preview to pique your interest:

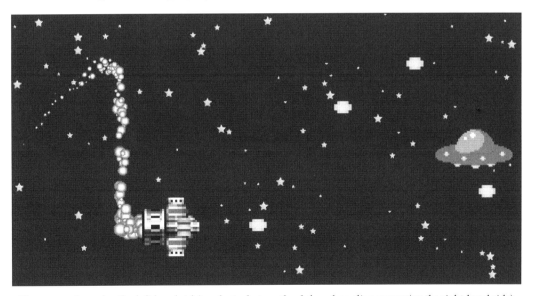

The game: player (on the left-hand side) seeks to destroy the defenseless alien saucer (on the right-hand side)

Building an app with lots of moving parts simultaneously presented on screen, especially a mobile (or multi-platform) game, depends heavily on a capable renderer. This is what we'll attempt to develop by the end of the book, partially based on the source code from the starfield screensaver discussed in *Chapter 8, Introducing Shaders*.

This chapter will also cover the following topics:

- Working with texture atlases in Kivy, complete with manual unpacking of texture coordinates for use in low-level code

- Further development of a GLSL-based particle system and usage of particle systems to create different in-game entities

- Implementing the game mechanics for a two-dimensional shooter — a control scheme suitable for mouse and touch screen, basic collision detection for bullets, and so on

As with all other code for this book, you can find the most up-to-date version of all source code on GitHub, at `https://github.com/mvasilkov/kb`. Consult the full source code of the application periodically when following along, because this puts things in context and makes the program flow more understandable.

Limitations of the project

The shoot-em-up game we're writing is going to be very minimal, feature-wise. In particular, here are the constraints:

- The whole motivational part (winning and game over conditions) is omitted for the sake of clarity. It should be easy to implement once you're happy with the gameplay.

- There's just one enemy type in our version of the game, and one simple movement pattern.

- Many opportunities for optimization were purposefully missed to make the code more concise and readable.

These are left as an exercise for the reader, if you're willing to do a bit more work. But first, let's review how texture maps work in Kivy — we'll rely on them later in the particle system code.

Texture atlases at a glance

Texture atlases (also known as sprite sheets) are a method of combining images used in the application into a larger composite texture. There are several advantages of doing so, compared to just loading a bunch of individual images like we did in previous projects:

- The application should open faster; it's usually cheaper to read one large file than several smaller ones. This may sound negligible until you have hundreds of textures, and then it becomes pretty noticeable—even more so over the network: HTTP requests add sizable overhead, which may become a deal breaker on mobile devices with constrained connectivity.

- Rendering is also subtly quicker when there's no need to rebind textures. Using a texture map effectively means that only the texture coordinates are affected by any change that would otherwise lead to switching textures.

- The previous point also makes atlases more suitable for use in situations when there's a single large model, such as our GLSL-based renderer. Again, texture coordinates are cheap and rebinding textures isn't.

 If you're coming from an HTML and CSS background, then you probably have heard about a very similar approach used in web development, called CSS sprites. The rationale is basically the same, sans the GLSL part. Since web apps are mostly delivered over the network, the gain from using CSS sprites is substantial even for a small number of images—every eliminated HTTP request counts.

In this section of the chapter, we'll review the following topics:

- Creating texture maps using Kivy's built-in CLI utility
- File format and structure of an `.atlas` file
- The usage of texture atlases in Kivy-based apps

If you're already familiar with Kivy atlases, feel free to skip straight to the *Ad hoc usage of atlases with GLSL* section.

Creating an atlas

Unlike in web development, where no standard tool has emerged for this particular task, Kivy framework comes with a useful command-line utility for texture maps. Its invocation looks like the following:

```
python -m kivy.atlas <atlas_name> <texture_size> <images...>
```

On a Mac, replace `python` with `kivy` — that's the conventional command provided by `Kivy.app` for invoking a Kivy-aware Python interpreter.

This creates two or more files, depending on whether all images fit into a single composite texture of requested size. For the purpose of this tutorial, we assume that the value of `texture_size` is large enough to include every last image.

All output files are named after the `atlas_name` argument that you provide on the command line:

- The atlas index will be called `<atlas_name>.atlas`
- Textures have an additional ordinal suffix — `<atlas_name>-0.png` (this one is always created), `<atlas_name>-1.png`, and so on

Atlas structure

An index of any given atlas, `.atlas`, is basically a **JavaScript Object Notation (JSON)** file describing the positioning of individual textures on the map. Its contents look like the following (formatted for readability):

```
{
    "game-0.png": {
        "player": [2, 170, 78, 84],
        "bullet": [82, 184, 24, 16]
    }
}
```

Textures are named after their corresponding source images, without an extension: a file `foo.png` becomes just `foo`. The numbers in each record describe a region of the large texture: `[x, y, width, height]`, where all values are in pixels.

A composite texture is about what you'd expect from a concatenation of images, as shown in the next figure. Usually, it will be tightly packed to efficiently utilize most of its area.

When creating an atlas, Kivy handles individual sprites' edges with precaution, accounting for possible rendering artifacts related to rounding. This is why one may notice extra pixels on the edges of a sprite. This effect isn't always visible, but when it is, don't worry — it's by design and serves a good cause.

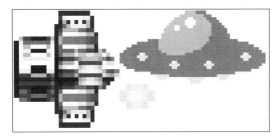

A texture atlas is merely a concatenation of smaller images

Using atlases in regular Kivy-based code is as simple as replacing file paths with a special protocol, `atlas:` (conceptually similar to `http:`). As you're already aware, the usual file reference in Kivy language looks similar to the next code snippet:

```
Image:
    source: 'flags/Israel.png'
```

An atlas reference, however, will use the following notation:

```
Image:
    source: 'atlas://flags/Israel'
```

Continue reading for a complete (albeit very simple) example of creating and using an atlas in a conventional Kivy app, a "hello world" of sorts.

Using Kivy atlases in an easy way

For the purpose of this example, let's borrow two icons from our previous projects and name them `icon_clock.png` and `icon_paint.png`:

Individual icons used to craft a sample atlas

To create an atlas, we crank open a terminal and issue the following command:

```
kivy -m kivy.atlas icons 512 icon_clock.png icon_paint.png
```

Remember to substitute the `kivy` command with `python` when not on a Mac. The `kivy.atlas` part, however, stays the same on all systems.

The atlas utility should reply with something along the lines of the following:

```
[INFO] Kivy v1.8.0
[INFO] [Atlas] create an 512x512 rgba image
('Atlas created at', 'icons.atlas')
1 image have been created
```

After a successful completion of the aforementioned command, a couple of new files—`icons.atlas` and `icons-0.png`—should have appeared in the same folder.

 At this point, it is safe to remove source images. It's advised that you still keep them around for the likely event that you'll need to rebuild the atlas later, for example, when adding new images or replacing existing ones.

The atlas is ready. As for the usage, we can create a simple demo app in a few lines of Python and the Kivy language.

The Python source, `basic.py`, contains a barebones Kivy app:

```python
from kivy.app import App

class BasicApp(App):
    pass

if __name__ == '__main__':
    BasicApp().run()
```

This is very simple and exists for the sole purpose of (automatically) loading the layout, defined in the `basic.kv` file. The accompanying Kivy language file reads as follows:

```
BoxLayout:
    orientation: 'horizontal'

    Image:
        source: 'atlas://icons/icon_clock'

    Image:
        source: 'atlas://icons/icon_paint'
```

This simple usage of an atlas results in the following layout, and it is pretty much what you'd expect from looking at the source code:

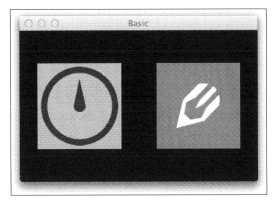

Basic usage of a Kivy atlas

As you can see, apart from the `atlas:` protocol described earlier, there is nothing new or intriguing in this example. So, let's move on to parsing texture atlases and their more advanced usage.

Ad hoc usage of atlases with GLSL

The built-in support for atlases in Kivy works just fine for simple cases, but not so much for our custom GLSL-based application, which manages all rendering, textures and whatnot, on its own.

Thankfully, the `.atlas` file format is JSON, which means we can easily parse it utilizing the `json` module from the Python standard library. Afterwards, we should be able to translate pixel coordinates given in the file to UV coordinates for use with OpenGL routines.

Since we know the absolute size of each texture, we can also effortlessly compute the vertices' positions relative to center of each sprite. This facilitates easy rendering of sprites in their "original form", keeping both the size and the aspect ratio intact.

Data structure for UV mapping

Put together, there are a lot of values per sprite. In order to keep things maintainable we can define a lightweight record type (a named tuple) to hold these together:

```
from collections import namedtuple

UVMapping = namedtuple('UVMapping', 'u0 v0 u1 v1 su sv')
```

If you're not familiar with named tuples in Python, from the user's perspective this amounts to basically the following logic-less type, similar in concept to a `struct` compositional type in C:

```python
class UVMapping:
    def __init__(self, u0, v0, u1, v1, su, sv):
        self.u0 = u0  # top left corner
        self.v0 = v0  # ---
        self.u1 = u1  # bottom right corner
        self.v1 = v1  # ---
        self.su = su  # equals to 0.5 * width
        self.sv = sv  # equals to 0.5 * height
```

Note that this code is purely illustrative, and the preceding `namedtuple()` definition does not actually expand to this—the user-facing interface, however, is similar.

The meaning of each field is given in the following table:

Field(s)	Description
`u0, v0`	UV coordinates of the sprite's top-left corner
`u1, v1`	UV coordinates of the sprite's bottom-right corner
`su`	Sprite width divided by 2; this value is useful when building an array of vertices
`sv`	Sprite height divided by 2; this is similar to the previous field

Named fields provide direct access to different values inside the record, which dramatically improves readability: `tup.v1` reads much better than `tup[3]`. At the same time, `UVMapping` is essentially a tuple, an immutable and memory-efficient data structure with all fields still accessible by index, should the need arise.

Writing an atlas loader

Now, let's write a function that makes happen everything that was discussed so far: JSON parsing, coordinates fixup, and so on. This function will also be used in the final program:

```python
import json
from kivy.core.image import Image

def load_atlas(atlas_name):
    with open(atlas_name, 'rb') as f:
        atlas = json.loads(f.read().decode('utf-8'))
```

```
tex_name, mapping = atlas.popitem()
tex = Image(tex_name).texture
tex_width, tex_height = tex.size

uvmap = {}
for name, val in mapping.items():
    x0, y0, w, h = val
    x1, y1 = x0 + w, y0 + h
    uvmap[name] = UVMapping(
        x0 / tex_width, 1 - y1 / tex_height,
        x1 / tex_width, 1 - y0 / tex_height,
        0.5 * w, 0.5 * h)

return tex, uvmap
```

 Keep in mind that we're supporting only the simplest case: an atlas with just one composite texture. This is probably the most useful configuration anyway, so this limitation shouldn't affect our code in the slightest, especially since the atlas generation is completely under our control.

We're reversing the ordinate axis since the coordinates are initially given in Kivy's coordinate system, and we're better off using the OpenGL's coordinate system with the origin at the top-left. Otherwise, sprites will be flipped upside down (which, by the way, isn't a problem for most sprites in our little game. This means that such bugs could have lived in the codebase for a long time—unnoticed and practically harmless).

The call to `load_atlas('icons.atlas')` returns both the composite texture loaded from `icons-0.png`, and the description of each texture included in the atlas:

```
>>> load_atlas('icons.atlas')

(<Texture size=(512, 512)...>,
 {'icon_paint': UVMapping(u0=0.2578125, v0=0.00390625,
                          u1=0.5078125, v1=0.25390625,
                          su=64.0, sv=64.0),
  'icon_clock': UVMapping(...)})
```

(Numbers obviously may differ in your case.)

This data format is sufficient to pick out individual sprites from the texture and render them on screen—and that's exactly what we'll do next.

Rendering sprites from atlas

Armed with the above function, let's hack together a variation of the previous demo that uses the same texture map with GLSL.

The source code, `tex_atlas.py`, is conceptually similar to simple GLSL examples from *Chapter 8, Introducing Shaders*. It makes use of the `load_atlas()` function to populate the array of vertices:

```python
from kivy.graphics import Mesh
from kivy.graphics.instructions import RenderContext
from kivy.uix.widget import Widget

class GlslDemo(Widget):
    def __init__(self, **kwargs):
        Widget.__init__(self, **kwargs)
        self.canvas = RenderContext(use_parent_projection=True)
        self.canvas.shader.source = 'tex_atlas.glsl'

        fmt = (
            (b'vCenter',     2, 'float'),
            (b'vPosition',   2, 'float'),
            (b'vTexCoords0', 2, 'float'),
        )

        texture, uvmap = load_atlas('icons.atlas')

        a = uvmap['icon_clock']
        vertices = (
            128, 128, -a.su, -a.sv, a.u0, a.v1,
            128, 128,  a.su, -a.sv, a.u1, a.v1,
            128, 128,  a.su,  a.sv, a.u1, a.v0,
            128, 128, -a.su,  a.sv, a.u0, a.v0,
        )
        indices = (0, 1, 2, 2, 3, 0)

        b = uvmap['icon_paint']
        vertices += (
            256, 256, -b.su, -b.sv, b.u0, b.v1,
            256, 256,  b.su, -b.sv, b.u1, b.v1,
            256, 256,  b.su,  b.sv, b.u1, b.v0,
            256, 256, -b.su,  b.sv, b.u0, b.v0,
        )
        indices += (4, 5, 6, 6, 7, 4)
```

```
with self.canvas:
    Mesh(fmt=fmt, mode='triangles',
         vertices=vertices, indices=indices,
         texture=texture)
```

The code essentially just copies the output data from `load_atlas()` to the `vertices` array, besides the usual GLSL initialization sequence. We pick two different records: `icon_clock` (stored as an `a` variable for brevity) and `icon_paint` (named `b`, similar to `a`), and then shove them into the array of vertices.

Our vertex format for this example is very minimal:

- **vCenter**: This is the location of the sprite on the screen. It should be the same value for all vertices of a given sprite
- **vPosition**: This is the vertex position relative to the center of the sprite, unaffected by the previous value
- **vTexCoords0**: This is the texture coordinates (UV) for each vertex. It determines which part of the large texture will be rendered.

From these, only the sprite location (first two columns of raw numbers in the listing) cannot be derived from the UV mapping; everything else comes from the `load_atlas()` call.

Here is the corresponding shader code, `tex_atlas.glsl`:

```
---vertex
$HEADER$

attribute vec2 vCenter;

void main(void)
{
    tex_coord0 = vTexCoords0;
    mat4 move_mat = mat4
        (1.0, 0.0, 0.0, vCenter.x,
         0.0, 1.0, 0.0, vCenter.y,
         0.0, 0.0, 1.0, 0.0,
         0.0, 0.0, 0.0, 1.0);
    vec4 pos = vec4(vPosition.xy, 0.0, 1.0) * move_mat;
    gl_Position = projection_mat * modelview_mat * pos;
}

---fragment
$HEADER$
```

```
void main(void)
{
    gl_FragColor = texture2D(texture0, tex_coord0);
}
```

This has only the minimal capabilities—positioning and texturing—baked in. A similar shader will be used in the final game, with an addition of the relative sizing attribute, `vScale`.

 If you don't understand what's going on in the shader code, go back to *Chapter 8, Introducing Shaders*: it holds a number of examples that you may find relevant to the discussion at hand.

The end result, however uninteresting it may look, is depicted here:

Rendering sprites from the atlas using GLSL

With this, we can move on to the development of a generic sprite-based particle system that will, in its turn, serve as a foundation for all in-game objects.

Designing a reusable particle system

In this section, we're going to write a particle system that will be later used to create pretty much everything in the game—spaceships, bullets, and so on. This is the generic approach used in situations where you have many similar objects on the screen with very little logic for movement and interaction.

This topic will capitalize on the previous chapter's code. In fact, the starfield screensaver from the previous chapter as a whole is a fine example of a particle system; however, it lacks the necessary configurability and cannot be easily repurposed. We're going to change that without significantly altering the GLSL and related code.

It's worth mentioning that the chosen approach—rendering textured quads for each particle—isn't the most optimal in terms of low-level rendering. On the plus side, it's very straightforward, easy to reason about, and compatible with any implementation of OpenGL that supports GLSL at all.

If you choose to learn OpenGL more systematically, you will probably want to replace quads with point sprites or do something similar in concept; these enhancements are out of the scope of this book.

Class hierarchy

The API of our particle system will consist of two classes: `PSWidget`, which does all rendering, and a lightweight `Particle` class to represent individual particles.

These will be tightly coupled by design, which is usually frowned upon in terms of classical OOP, but improves performance considerably in our case: particles will access the vertices array in the renderer directly in order to alter the mesh—less copying in this case, taking into account that many particles will be active at the same time, can be a huge win.

The implementation of the particle system widget isn't substantially different from other GLSL-based widgets we've seen so far, except for the fact that now it's meant to be subclassed for actual use. Both `PSWidget` and `Particle` are abstract base classes, that is, they cannot be instantiated directly by calling, for example, `PSWidget()`.

There are different ways to enforce this restriction. We could have used the `abc` module from the Python standard library in order to create *true* abstract base classes (`abc` actually stands for just that). While this may be deemed useful by Java programmers and the like, it's not the approach routinely taken by Python developers.

For the sake of simplicity, we're going to write appropriate placeholders (stubs) raising `NotImplementedError` for all methods that require overriding. This will make the base class technically unusable without the use of metaclasses and complex inheritance, as the `abc` module suggests.

The PSWidget renderer class

Without further introduction, let's take a look at the creation of `PSWidget`:

```python
class PSWidget(Widget):
    indices = []
    vertices = []
    particles = []

    def __init__(self, **kwargs):
        Widget.__init__(self, **kwargs)
        self.canvas = RenderContext(use_parent_projection=True)
        self.canvas.shader.source = self.glsl

        self.vfmt = (
            (b'vCenter', 2, 'float'),
            (b'vScale', 1, 'float'),
            (b'vPosition', 2, 'float'),
            (b'vTexCoords0', 2, 'float'),
        )

        self.vsize = sum(attr[1] for attr in self.vfmt)

        self.texture, self.uvmap = load_atlas(self.atlas)
```

This is essentially the same familiar initialization we've seen in all GLSL examples, with some fields left undefined (they are borrowed from the subclass, which has to set these). The `self.glsl` property will hold the filename of the shader, and `self.atlas` is the filename of the texture map that will serve as the only source of textures for this renderer instance.

Note how we don't populate the vertices array here: this work is left for the subclass to do. We should, however, provide an easy way for descendant classes to work with our internal data structures. Hence, the following `PSWidget` method that makes it easy to add a large number of similar particles is used:

```python
def make_particles(self, Cls, num):
    count = len(self.particles)
    uv = self.uvmap[Cls.tex_name]

    for i in range(count, count + num):
        j = 4 * i
        self.indices.extend((
            j, j + 1, j + 2, j + 2, j + 3, j))
```

```
            self.vertices.extend((
                0, 0, 1, -uv.su, -uv.sv, uv.u0, uv.v1,
                0, 0, 1,  uv.su, -uv.sv, uv.u1, uv.v1,
                0, 0, 1,  uv.su,  uv.sv, uv.u1, uv.v0,
                0, 0, 1, -uv.su,  uv.sv, uv.u0, uv.v0,
            ))

            p = Cls(self, i)
            self.particles.append(p)
```

This instantiates the requested number of particles (num) of class Cls, adding them to the widget's self.particles list and populating self.vertices at the same time. Each particle type should expose a tex_name property that is used to look up the correct sprite in the UV mapping, the data structure derived earlier from the atlas (PSWidget.uvmap).

Strictly speaking, this helper function is optional, but very useful. Calls to this method will be included in the initialization of the widget's concrete class before rendering.

The last part of the widget base class is the rendering:

```
    def update_glsl(self, nap):
        for p in self.particles:
            p.advance(nap)
            p.update()

        self.canvas.clear()

        with self.canvas:
            Mesh(fmt=self.vfmt, mode='triangles',
                    indices=self.indices, vertices=self.vertices,
                    texture=self.texture)
```

Starting from the canvas.clear() call, this is just about the same code used in all GLSL-based examples. The beginning of the function is more interesting. We iterate through all particles and call two methods on each: the advance() method computes new state of the particle (it's up to the particle to decide what this does, not necessarily resembling any visible change), and update() keeps the necessary data in the array of vertices in sync with the internal state, if any.

Such separation of concerns, while not ideal for performance, helps readability somewhat. When (if) optimizing, first consider the following points:

- This loop can and should be parallelized, in full or partially
- This code can also run on another thread completely, and not update every frame (again, this optimization may apply to selected classes of particles, for example, stuff in background that doesn't affect main program flow)

These methods, along with other implementation details of particles, are described in the forthcoming sections.

The Particle class

In the following code we review yet another base class, `Particle`, that represents individual sprites. It resembles the `Star` class from the starfield project, sans the logic for movement (this will be implemented later by subclasses):

```python
class Particle:
    x = 0
    y = 0
    size = 1

    def __init__(self, parent, i):
        self.parent = parent
        self.vsize = parent.vsize
        self.base_i = 4 * i * self.vsize
        self.reset(created=True)

    def update(self):
        for i in range(self.base_i,
                       self.base_i + 4 * self.vsize,
                       self.vsize):
            self.parent.vertices[i:i + 3] = (
                self.x, self.y, self.size)

    def reset(self, created=False):
        raise NotImplementedError()

    def advance(self, nap):
        raise NotImplementedError()
```

Storing a reference to the *parent* PSWidget in the constructor allows us to interface with it later on. This primarily happens in the update() method, also shown in the previous listing—it makes changes to all four vertices of a polygon to keep those in sync with the particle's desired location and scale (x, y, and size properties).

There is at least one method in this new class that wasn't present in the Star class, namely, advance(). This one has to be overridden, since there's no default behavior for advancing the scene. It's up to a particle to decide how it should change with time. As you will see shortly, particle systems can be used to create substantially different effects.

The reset() method is called to reinitialize a particle that ended its life cycle (for example, has left the screen or exhausted its TTL). It's highly particle system-specific, but generally any such system has some notion of a particle being restored to a blank or randomized initial state. Again, there is no clever default behavior we could invoke here, so there's only a stub in place.

Raising NotImplementedError from a virtual method is a way to inform the developer that it would be nice to define this method on a derived class. We could have omitted the last two methods altogether, but that would lead to a less relevant error, AttributeError. Preserving method signatures, even in the absence of a default implementation, is also nice and reduces guesswork for your peers (or your future self, should you revisit the same code after a long delay).

The idea behind the new keyword argument, created, which is passed to reset(), is simple. Some particle systems may need an additional (or merely different) initialization routine when particles first spawn. A good example of such behavior is the new starfield (we will get to it shortly), where stars spawn on the right-hand side of the screen. If we don't account for the *just created* state, then all stars will indeed appear on the rightmost edge of the screen with the same x coordinate and thus form a straight line. This graphical glitch is clearly undesirable, so we fully randomize the location of stars if created is set to True, which gives us nice initial distribution.

Calls to reset() will clearly mean subsequent respawning of particles much more often than the first-time initialization, so the created flag defaults to False.

We're pretty much done with the base classes at this point. As you will see shortly, the implementation of the game itself becomes very straightforward as soon as *hard* technical details are abstracted out. For the rest of the chapter, we'll employ particle system basics outlined here in creative ways to build various stuff, from background to interactive in-game objects such as bullets.

Writing the game

Our application is structured around building blocks described earlier: our root widget is a PSWidget subclass called Game and all in-game entities will derive from the Particle class.

Here is the short and sweet base application:

```
from kivy.base import EventLoop
from kivy.clock import Clock

class Game(PSWidget):
    glsl = 'game.glsl'
    atlas = 'game.atlas'

    def initialize(self):
        pass

class GameApp(App):
    def build(self):
        EventLoop.ensure_window()
        return Game()

    def on_start(self):
        self.root.initialize()
        Clock.schedule_interval(
            self.root.update_glsl, 60 ** -1)
```

The following are the details about external files referenced here:

- The game.glsl shader file is the same as starfield.glsl from the previous chapter

- The game.atlas texture map hosts the following textures:

    ○ star: This texture resembles a star, similar to the one we've used in the previous project

    ○ player: This is a spaceship facing to the right (in the general direction of movement)

    ○ trail: This is a *fireball* (a single particle of flame) emitted from ship's rocket engine

    ○ bullet: This is a projectile spawned by ship's imaginary frontal cannon

    ○ ufo: This is an alien saucer, facing to the left (and moving against the current)

The previous code renders nothing on screen yet, since we haven't populated the vertices array. Let's start from the background and implement the stars first.

Implementing stars

Once again we build a simple star-field. This time it scrolls right-to-left to imitate movement, similar in concept to the Kivy Bird game that we built earlier.

To create a simple parallax effect (just like in Kivy Bird), we assign stars to three planes and then set their size and speed to match. Stars on a plane with a greater number are bigger and move faster than those from a lesser plane. The moment a star goes off the screen, it's reborn at random position on a random plane.

Let's review the particle system code implementing the new and improved starfield:

```python
from random import randint, random

class Star(Particle):
    plane = 1
    tex_name = 'star'

    def reset(self, created=False):
        self.plane = randint(1, 3)

        if created:
            self.x = random() * self.parent.width
        else:
            self.x = self.parent.width

        self.y = random() * self.parent.height
        self.size = 0.1 * self.plane

    def advance(self, nap):
        self.x -= 20 * self.plane * nap
        if self.x < 0:
            self.reset()
```

The `tex_name` property is required and refers to a texture inside `game.atlas`.

Resetting randomizes a star's plane and position, depending on whether the method was called during the initialization (`created=True`) or not; the rationale for this was described earlier.

The last method, `advance()`, is simple: move the sprite to the left until it's out of screen, and then reset it.

In order to put our new particle system to use, we need to add a number of stars using the `make_particles()` helper from `PSWidget`. This happens in `Game.initialize()`:

```
def initialize(self):
    self.make_particles(Star, 200)
```

Finally, some visible fruits of our labor:

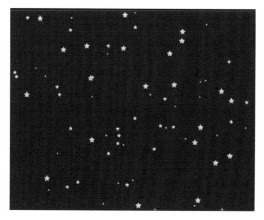

The starfield, revisited

Making a spaceship

We need exactly one spaceship at all times (since we're building a single-player game), which means that the implementation will be a degenerate case of a particle system having just one particle. This is done for the sake of unification with the rest of the code. There is nothing we could gain by architecting this particular object differently.

The player's spacecraft will be glued to the pointer location at all times. To achieve this effect, we store the position of the pointer in a pair of `Game` properties, namely `player_x` and `player_y`, and then put the spaceship sprite at those coordinates when updating the scene. To save the pointer location, we can use the following code:

```
from kivy.core.window import Window

class Game(PSWidget):
    def update_glsl(self, nap):
        self.player_x, self.player_y = Window.mouse_pos

        PSWidget.update_glsl(self, nap)
```

Since the spaceship is under player's complete control, there is no other logic that we could implement in the particle class — apart from just moving the sprite to the last pointer position accordingly:

```
class Player(Particle):
    tex_name = 'player'

    def reset(self, created=False):
        self.x = self.parent.player_x
        self.y = self.parent.player_y

    advance = reset
```

As you can see, `reset()` and `advance()` methods are the same. There is just about nothing else we can do.

Don't forget to actually spawn a particle of this type:

```
def initialize(self):
    self.make_particles(Star, 200)
    self.make_particles(Player, 1)
```

The end result so far resembles a lone spacecraft in the middle of an endless void:

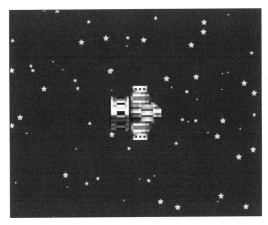

The spaceship follows the mouse,
putting the user in direct control

Creating a trail of fire

Every respectable spacecraft in a sci-fi setting is followed by a flaming trail. Particles composing such a trail use the following algorithm:

1. A particle spawns near the engine, its size randomized. The size of the particle is also its **time to live** (TTL).

2. It then travels away from the spacecraft at a constant speed, shrinking in size while doing so.

3. Particles that have shrunk to about 10 percent of the normal size are reset and begin their journey anew.

Given many particles, this effect may look nice in motion. Sadly, screenshots cannot convey the dynamics, so be sure to run the example code to get a better impression.

Long story short, the particle system implementation is given as follows:

```python
class Trail(Particle):
    tex_name = 'trail'

    def reset(self, created=False):
        self.x = self.parent.player_x + randint(-30, -20)
        self.y = self.parent.player_y + randint(-10, 10)

        if created:
            self.size = 0
        else:
            self.size = random() + 0.6

    def advance(self, nap):
        self.size -= nap
        if self.size <= 0.1:
            self.reset()
        else:
            self.x -= 120 * nap
```

This implements the aforementioned algorithm quite literally, while relying on the same `player_x` and `player_y` properties to determine the current position of the ship.

As mentioned earlier, we should assign many particles to the effect so that it looks good:

```python
def initialize(self):
    self.make_particles(Star, 200)
    self.make_particles(Trail, 200)
    self.make_particles(Player, 1)
```

Here is the screenshot of the result:

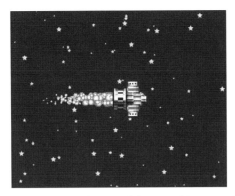

Fire burning in vacuum: looks neat while not making a case for realism

The last two particle systems that remain unimplemented, namely enemies and bullets, are different. Unlike other classes of particles we've seen previously, where all instances are being displayed simultaneously at any given time, neither bullets nor enemies spawn all at once; both wait for a special event to occur and then increase the *population* of objects by one, firing a bullet or spawning a single enemy.

Nevertheless, we want to allocate a fixed number of such particles in advance, because growing and shrinking the array of vertices unnecessarily complicates the code and is not desirable.

The catch is to add a new Boolean field to a particle to signify whether it's active (shown on screen) or not, and then *activate* such particles on demand. This approach will be demonstrated shortly.

Making bullets

We want our ship's cannon to fire while we're holding a mouse button or touching the screen continuously. This setup is easy to implement using the newly added `firing` property to denote that the trigger is being pulled:

```
class Game(PSWidget):
    firing = False
    fire_delay = 0

    def on_touch_down(self, touch):
        self.firing = True
        self.fire_delay = 0

    def on_touch_up(self, touch):
        self.firing = False
```

To add a brief delay between shots, we introduce yet another property, `fire_delay`. This variable decreases each frame until it reaches zero, then a new bullet spawns and `fire_delay` is incremented. The cycle continues while `firing` is `True`:

```
def update_glsl(self, nap):
    self.player_x, self.player_y = Window.mouse_pos

    if self.firing:
        self.fire_delay -= nap

    PSWidget.update_glsl(self, nap)
```

Now, let's see the aforementioned active state of a particle. Initially, all bullets are inactive (that is, `active=False`) and removed from the screen (the coordinates `x=-100, y=-100` are set for the bullets, which effectively prevents them from rendering). The code is as follows:

```
class Bullet(Particle):
    active = False
    tex_name = 'bullet'

    def reset(self, created=False):
        self.active = False
        self.x = -100
        self.y = -100
```

When looping over bullets, we skip those that are inactive, unless `firing_delay` has reached zero. In this case, we activate one bullet and put it in front of the player, bumping the `firing_delay` variable to reset the countdown.

Active bullets move just like stars, albeit in the opposite direction. Unlike stars, bullets that go off screen don't auto-respawn. They return to the inactive pool instead, vanishing from view. The code is as follows:

```
def advance(self, nap):
    if self.active:
        self.x += 250 * nap
        if self.x > self.parent.width:
            self.reset()

    elif (self.parent.firing and
            self.parent.fire_delay <= 0):
        self.active = True
        self.x = self.parent.player_x + 40
        self.y = self.parent.player_y
        self.parent.fire_delay += 0.3333
```

The `fire_delay` property set to one-third of a second, which obviously leads to an average rate of automatic fire of three **rounds per second (RPS)**.

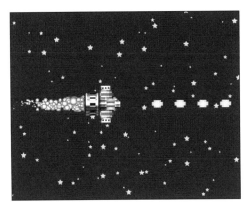

A spacecraft with guns blazing

Implementing enemies

Enemies are conceptually similar to bullets, but since they spawn continuously, we don't need a flag such as `firing`—a `spawn_delay` property is sufficient. This is, by the way, the final evolution of the `update_glsl()` method:

```
class Game(PSWidget):
    spawn_delay = 1

    def update_glsl(self, nap):
        self.player_x, self.player_y = Window.mouse_pos

        if self.firing:
            self.fire_delay -= nap

        self.spawn_delay -= nap

        PSWidget.update_glsl(self, nap)
```

During the initialization, we create a predefined number of enemies, initially inactive. In order to implement collision detection with bullets later on, we also store a list of bullets (a slice of the `Game.particles` list) separately:

```
def initialize(self):
    self.make_particles(Star, 200)
    self.make_particles(Trail, 200)
    self.make_particles(Player, 1)
```

```
self.make_particles(Enemy, 25)
self.make_particles(Bullet, 25)

self.bullets = self.particles[-25:]
```

The corresponding particle class will be the most complex so far, mainly because of the more involved movement pattern. In addition to a constant movement speed along the x axis, each enemy also features randomized vertical movement vector, v. When a particle of this type is about to leave the screen from the top or bottom edge, the particle's v property changes its sign accordingly, reflecting the enemy back into the visible screen space.

Other rules are similar to how bullets work: when an enemy reaches the opposite edge of the screen, it resets and effectively disappears until spawned again. The code is as follows:

```
class Enemy(Particle):
    active = False
    tex_name = 'ufo'
    v = 0

    def reset(self, created=False):
        self.active = False
        self.x = -100
        self.y = -100
        self.v = 0

    def advance(self, nap):
        if self.active:
            if self.check_hit():  # Step 1
                self.reset()
                return

            self.x -= 200 * nap  # Step 2
            if self.x < -50:
                self.reset()
                return

            self.y += self.v * nap  # Step 3
            if self.y <= 0:
                self.v = abs(self.v)
            elif self.y >= self.parent.height:
                self.v = -abs(self.v)
```

```
        elif self.parent.spawn_delay <= 0:   # Step 4
            self.active = True
            self.x = self.parent.width + 50
            self.y = self.parent.height * random()
            self.v = randint(-100, 100)
            self.parent.spawn_delay += 1
```

This listing may appear relatively long but the algorithm is actually pretty simple to grasp:

1. Check whether we're hit by a bullet and reset (see the next section).

2. Move horizontally, check whether we have left the view, and reset.

3. Move vertically, check whether we're leaving the view, and change the vector sign.

4. Spawn another enemy if `spawn_delay` has ended and bump `spawn_delay`.

Collision detection

Another interesting aspect of the `Enemy` class that we haven't seen before is the `check_hit()` method. There are two things enemies can collide with: the player's spaceship and bullets. For the sake of simplicity, let's say that the protagonist is invincible and the collision simply destroys the enemy; a colliding bullet, however, also despawns. The code is as follows:

```
def check_hit(self):
    if math.hypot(self.parent.player_x - self.x,
                  self.parent.player_y - self.y) < 60:
        return True

    for b in self.parent.bullets:
        if not b.active:
            continue

        if math.hypot(b.x - self.x, b.y - self.y) < 30:
            b.reset()
            return True
```

This collision detection routine is as simple as possible: `math.hypot()` merely computes distance between center points, so we assume that all objects are approximately round for the purpose of this check. We also don't try to collide with inactive bullets for obvious reasons—logically inactive entities don't exist and physically they are located outside the visible screen space anyway. So, they probably don't collide with objects on screen.

This concludes the first (barely) playable version of the game.

Enemies sighted

Finishing touches

There are many areas where this game can and should be improved, particularly in terms of gameplay. It goes without saying that this prototype, as it stands, isn't marketable.

Some suggestions for *homework*, should you be interested in working on this project further, are listed here:

- First of all, the game needs a "game over" state, badly. Winning is optional, but losing is a must; otherwise, it's just not competitive at all, like an interactive screensaver.

- Another obvious improvement is adding content—diversity is king. More enemies, more attack patterns, and probably the ability for selected enemies to shoot back at player. A progressive increase in difficulty level goes in the same bucket: later stages of the game should bring bigger waves of enemies, faster spawn times, and so on.

- Adding sound effects is probably the simplest enhancement. Refer to *Chapter 7, Writing a Flappy Bird Clone*, for details. The same `MultiAudio` class can be trivially reused in this project too. Alternatively, take a look at the sample code accompanying this chapter.

Summary

The main point of this chapter is that a particle system can be used for vastly different things. Perhaps this is not the most stunningly clever idea you've heard today, so let's instead summarize the main points of the whole book, regardless of small implementation details.

In this lengthy write-up, we barely scratched the surface of what can be easily done with Python and Kivy. The realm of possibilities is vast and diverse:

- Utility apps for desktop and mobile

- Applications for content creation, be it a graphical or text editor, possibly even a sound synthesizer

- Networked apps used for chatting, other ways of social networking, and remote control programs

- Video games

Over the course of this book, we also highlighted some useful principles of working with any new technology efficiently:

- Apply your experience from other problem domains, such as web development. Kivy is different, but it's not that much different; many approaches are actually reusable between substantially different environments.

- Attempt to understand what's happening behind the scenes. Understanding the inner workings of the framework will help immensely when debugging.

- Related to the previous point, if docs are missing or unclear, read the source code. It's Python after all, so naturally it's very readable.

- Don't hesitate to search the Web for solutions to problems and topics of interest. More often than not, someone already had this problem and found a workaround.

All in all, I sincerely hope you enjoyed the ride. If you have any questions or want to discuss something, by all means contact me at `mvasilkov@gmail.com` (and expect excruciatingly slow replies!).

The Python Ecosystem

This book doesn't attempt to answer all the questions that you might have had about Kivy, or exemplify every remotely possible approach to writing a Kivy app; it should instead serve as a practical, hands-on introduction to writing various programs with a user interface in Python.

Kivy's major achievement is bridging the gap between a Python toolchain and mobile app development on Android and iOS. Unlike bindings to Qt (PyQt and PySide), Kivy is inherently Pythonic (apart from minor implementation details such as the `Window` object). These two aspects alone make Kivy a viable option to consider when writing your next user-facing application.

This notwithstanding, I strongly encourage you to explore the vast Python ecosystem. It just so happens that a great many Python modules manage to stay under the radar. Kivy is actually one of them, overshadowed by, for example, the relatively more popular Qt framework (they clearly don't belong in the same ballpark, but a common misconception is that these are mostly interchangeable, for reasons unclear).

The following annotated list contains a few interesting Python modules, both well-known and relatively obscure. This may serve as an inspiration for writing a new app, or merely as an illustration of the riches found in the Python biome. Obviously, this list is far from complete, or even extensive: you will certainly uncover many other unique libraries and tools over the course of your Python career.

So here it is, a highly subjective enumeration of selected, downright amazing Python packages, in no particular order:

- **Requests**: This module is a well-known, über-useful HTTP package with readable, consistent interface. It greatly simplifies writing all sorts of HTTP clients.

- **Pyjnius**: Discussed in slightly more detail in *Chapter 3*, *Sound Recorder for Android*, this module provides a seamless and relatively lightweight Java interoperability layer. This tool lets you reuse any Java library, on Android and desktop, from the comfort of your Python environment. Needless to say, Java libraries (of equivocal usefulness) come in great numbers, so Pyjnius may prove useful on many occasions.

- **mitmproxy (man-in-the-middle proxy)**: This is a toolkit for capturing and editing HTTP traffic. Possible uses for mitmproxy include debugging and testing network applications, security auditing, and otherwise toying with unsuspecting programs. It can be also exploited as a network screen for filtering traffic; this particular use case is popular with governments these days. Might land you a job with the KGB, or not.

- **music21**: This is a toolkit for computer-aided musicology developed at MIT that provides a way to work with symbolic music data. It allows you to read, write, and manipulate musical scores, conduct complex musical and statistical analysis on a representative corpus of classical music, fiddle with algorithmic composition, and so on.

- **Pydub**: This is a library for audio manipulation with a consistent, Pythonic interface. It allows you to perform a number of audio editing tasks, such as slicing, concatenating, crossfading, and so on. Pydub uses ffmpeg for transcoding, which means it supports most popular file formats out of the box.

- **Django**: This is an undoubtedly popular web framework for building dynamic, database-backed websites. What many people don't suspect, however, is that Django can also be used for many other, barely related, tasks that include the following:

  - Making powerful command-line tools for database manipulation, using Django models and **object-relational mapping (ORM)**

  - Employing the excellent Django's template engine for pretty much anything that requires a template engine

  - Building static websites

- **RenPy (stylized as Ren'Py)**: This is a visual novel engine, used for professional game development. Visual novels, once practically unheard of outside Japan, are becoming more popular now, with selected RenPy-powered titles readily available for consumption on the AppStore, Google Play, Steam, and via other software distribution channels.

NumPy, SciPy, IPython, and so on were purposefully omitted from the preceding list; they are so pervasive that there is hardly any need to reintroduce them.

If you find this topic mildly interesting and would like to learn more, there are a few websites that might be useful:

- Awesome Python, a curated list of awesome Python software is available at `https://github.com/vinta/awesome-python#awesome-python`
- The Hitchhiker's Guide to Python is an opinionated handbook of Python best practices, covering many interrelated topics. It is located at `http://docs.python-guide.org/en/latest/#scenario-guide`
- PyMOTW, the Python Module of the Week series by Doug Hellmann, can be found at `http://pymotw.com/2/contents.html`
- Last but not least, the official Python wiki hosts a directory of useful packages at `https://wiki.python.org/moin/UsefulModules`

The multitude of packages that provide practical solutions to real-world problems is a defining characteristic of today's Python programming. Code reuse is great, so in no event should you hesitate to borrow from the rich Python ecosystem and to give back when (if) that's feasible.

As a direct consequence of the preceding discussion, Python expands your toolbelt with many things that are universally considered non-trivial. This includes a certain subset of scientific computations, secure and scalable web servers, network services, fast hardware-accelerated graphics, and so on.

This is a valid reason to choose Python for your next project, and it also gives some insight into why many great projects loaded with powerful features—such as Kivy—are written in Python (and related languages, for example, RPython).

The moral of the story: know your ecosystem and it will pay off immensely by shouldering a lot of hard work, making you more productive and your hair soft and silky. *Because having a right tool for the job is indispensable.*

Index

R

rapid application development (RAD) 38
raster images 76
Remote Desktop app
  creating 117
  JavaScript client, developing 126
  Kivy Remote Desktop app 131
  server 119
RenPy (Ren'Py) 253
repetition
  named classes 27
  reducing 25-27
Requests library
  URL 138
reusable particle system
  class hierarchy 233
  designing 232
root widget 39
rounds per second (RPS) 245

S

scalable vector icons
  about 75
  icon fonts 75
  icon font, using in Kivy 77-79
  raster images 76
screen
  canvas, clearing 51, 52
  clearing 49, 50
  events, passing 50, 51
  time, updating on 21, 22
  touches, displaying on 47-49
screen manager
  about 98, 99
  animation, customizing 100, 101
  chatroom screen layout 103, 104
  login screen layout 101-103
server, Remote Desktop app
  about 119
  advanced server functionality 121-123
  clicks, emulating 124, 125
  Flask, installing 119
  Flask web server 120, 121
server source code 94
shoot-em-up game
  limitations 222

Simple DirectMedia Layer (SDL) 43
sound
  playing 88
  recording 85, 86
sound effects, Flappy Bird game
  adding 192
  Kivy sound playback 191
  producing 190, 191
sound, recording
  permissions 87, 88
spaceship, game
  creating 240
special syntax 114, 115
sprites
  rendering, from atlas 230-232
Starfield app
  application structure 214
  corresponding GLSL, writing 218, 219
  creating 213
  data structures 214, 217
  initializers 214-216
  scene, advancing 217, 218
Starfield class 214
stars, game
  implementing 239
stopwatch
  controls 34, 35
  placing 33
  time, formatting for 32
storage classes, GLSL
  attribute 206
  uniform 206
  varying 206
storage path, native API
  about 83, 84
  logs, reading from device 84
strftime formatting essentials
  %B 22
  %d 22
  %H 22
  %I 22
  %m 22
  %M 22
  %S 22
  %Y 22
strftime function
  limitations 32

Thank you for buying
Kivy Blueprints

About Packt Publishing

Packt, pronounced 'packed', published its first book, *Mastering phpMyAdmin for Effective MySQL Management*, in April 2004, and subsequently continued to specialize in publishing highly focused books on specific technologies and solutions.

Our books and publications share the experiences of your fellow IT professionals in adapting and customizing today's systems, applications, and frameworks. Our solution-based books give you the knowledge and power to customize the software and technologies you're using to get the job done. Packt books are more specific and less general than the IT books you have seen in the past. Our unique business model allows us to bring you more focused information, giving you more of what you need to know, and less of what you don't.

Packt is a modern yet unique publishing company that focuses on producing quality, cutting-edge books for communities of developers, administrators, and newbies alike. For more information, please visit our website at www.packtpub.com.

About Packt Open Source

In 2010, Packt launched two new brands, Packt Open Source and Packt Enterprise, in order to continue its focus on specialization. This book is part of the Packt Open Source brand, home to books published on software built around open source licenses, and offering information to anybody from advanced developers to budding web designers. The Open Source brand also runs Packt's Open Source Royalty Scheme, by which Packt gives a royalty to each open source project about whose software a book is sold.

Writing for Packt

We welcome all inquiries from people who are interested in authoring. Book proposals should be sent to author@packtpub.com. If your book idea is still at an early stage and you would like to discuss it first before writing a formal book proposal, then please contact us; one of our commissioning editors will get in touch with you.

We're not just looking for published authors; if you have strong technical skills but no writing experience, our experienced editors can help you develop a writing career, or simply get some additional reward for your expertise.

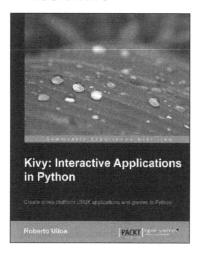

Kivy: Interactive Applications in Python

ISBN: 978-1-78328-159-6   Paperback: 138 pages

Create cross-platform UI/UX applications and games in Python

1. Use Kivy to implement apps and games in Python that run on multiple platforms.

2. Discover how to build a User Interface (UI) through the Kivy Language.

3. Glue the UI components with the logic of the applications through events and the powerful Kivy properties.

4. Detect gestures, create animations, and schedule tasks.

Mastering UDK Game Development HOTSHOT

ISBN: 978-1-84969-560-2   Paperback: 290 pages

Eight projects specifically designed to help you exploit the Unreal Development Kit to its full potential

1. Guides you through advanced projects that help augment your skills with UDK by practical example.

2. Comes complete with all the art assets and additional resources that you need to create stunning content.

3. Perfect for level designers who want to take their skills to the next level.

Please check **www.PacktPub.com** for information on our titles

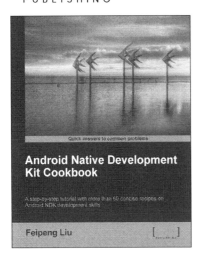

Made in the USA
Coppell, TX
01 August 2020